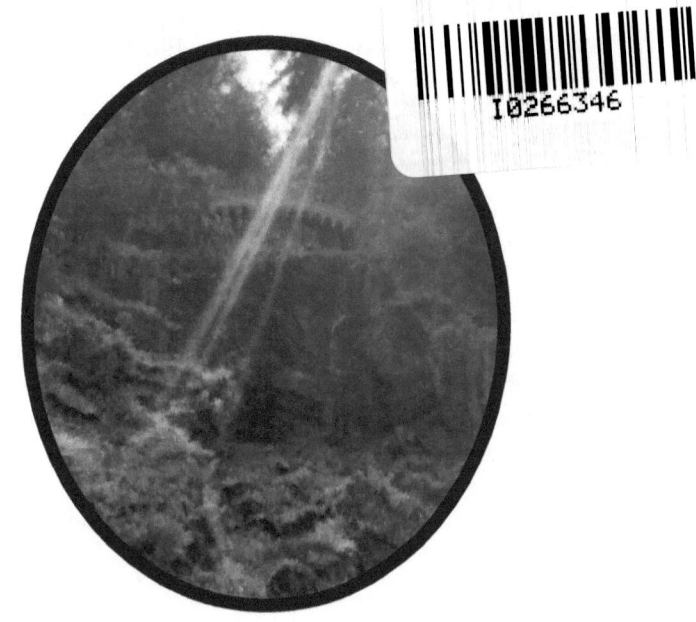

BOOK OF HOURS, BOOK OF DAYS AND NIGHTS

SELECTED POEMS

E. L. RISDEN

ANAPHORA LITERARY PRESS

QUANAH, TEXAS

Anaphora Literary Press
1108 W 3rd Street
Quanah, TX 79252
https://anaphoraliterary.com

Book design by Anna Faktorovich, Ph.D.

Copyright © 2018 by E. L. Risden

All rights reserved. No part of this book may be reproduced in any form or by any electronic or mechanical means, including information storage and retrieval systems, without permission in writing from E. L. Risden. Writers are welcome to quote brief passages in their critical studies, as American copyright law dictates.

Printed in the United States of America, United Kingdom and in Australia on acid-free paper.

Published in 2018 by Anaphora Literary Press

Book of Hours, Book of Days and Nights: Selected Poems
E. L. Risden—1st edition.

Library of Congress Control Number: 2018907666

Library Cataloging Information

Risden, E. L., 1957-, author.
    Book of hours, book of days and nights : Selected poems / E. L. Risden
    158 p. ; 9 in.
    ISBN 978-1-68114-457-3 (softcover : alk. paper)
    ISBN 978-1-68114-458-0 (hardcover : alk. paper)
    ISBN 978-1-68114-459-7 (e-book)
1. Poetry—American—General. 2. Poetry—Subjects & Themes—Nature.
3. Music—Lyrics.
PN6099-6110: Collections of general literature: Poetry
811: American poetry in English

BOOK OF HOURS, BOOK OF DAYS AND NIGHTS

SELECTED POEMS

E. L. Risden

CONTENTS

Preface	7
Book of Hours	9
Book of Days and Nights	33
Women of Middle-earth	73
Senryu Sequence	90
Chaucer the Vintner	95
from *On Shakespeare, In Sonnets*	113
from *Songs of the City*	118
from *Among Dusty Shelves*	123
from *Light on Stone*	128
from *A Second City Street Prophet Sings the Blues*	133
from *The Streets of Harmon Falls*	140
from *Through a Glass Darkly*	152
Postscript	156

Preface

At some point most writers, especially poets, I suspect, feel a need or desire to assemble a volume of collected or selected works.

While not a poet by trade, I've been writing (and rewriting) poems as an avocation since my early teens, that is, for more than forty-five years now. I still continue to indulge myself, both as part of my teaching and simply for fun, or because now and then a poem seems to me the best way to communicate something I want to say. Poems make us concentrate language and thought.

One practical reason for a collection stands out: the poet then has a volume to use for readings and perhaps to sell. Ego may come into play—in this case I hope not. But, perhaps especially for current academics, one may feel an urge to assess the body of work up to that time. Have my poems evolved and changed? Have I got somewhere better than where I started?

W. H. Auden wrote that a great danger comes with writing too good a poem too early in one's career: the poet then spends the rest of his or her writing life re-writing that same poem rather than moving on to something new. While evolution means *change*, not necessarily improvement, we want, I think, both to evolve and to improve. We realize that not every poem will live up to our hopes for it, but we want to believe that by practicing our craft and by living an attentive life we can, at least now and then, make better poems. So this volume embodies a practical attempt to package materials for readings, to assess what I've done up to this point in my life, to consider how to get better, and also to assemble a record of a learning process, hoping that the collection may reach a few readers who find pleasure in it and inspiration for and ways to think about their own work.

Some of the poems here have appeared in print or online before, but some are now reaching publication for the first time. The two sequences named in the title, The "Book of Hours" and the "Book of Days," represent new assemblies, though a few of the poems have got into print before. The "Women of Middle-earth" sequence (obviously inspired by J. R. R. Tolkien) came from a request to several poets by Professor Eileen Moore of Cleveland State University who has over a number of years created a song-cycle from some of our poems; her music far outstrips my poems, but I thank her sincerely for including those of mine she has, and I have added a few other "characters" beyond those poems that she has set so deftly to music. The *senryu* sequence was originally to form part of a student/faculty project that never reached completion. The brief "Chaucer the Vintner" series includes poems that come incidentally from the practice of one of my scholarly interests, *medievalism*, the use of materials from the Middle Ages by later writers. The Postscript is, as Freud might say, simply a postscript.

    I've selected poems from the books and chapbooks I've published so far (*On Shakespeare, In Sonnets* from Cambridge Scholars Press; *A Second City Street Prophet Sings the Blues* and *Through a Glass Darkly* from Mellen Poetry Press; *The Streets of Harmon Falls* from The Troy Book Makers; *Light on Stone*, Cassandra Press; *Among Dusty Shelves*, East Coast Editions; *Songs of the City*, Demosthenes Press), trying to get the most representative samples from each. Some published individually in literary magazines or nonce publications find inclusion here: my thanks to all those editors and publishers who have supported my efforts. Thanks especially to those of you who now have this book in hand and are offering some of your irreplaceable living time to read it. I hope the poems reward your gift.

BOOK OF HOURS

Bookshelves

Incunabula like neat-bound minds…
Tomes, piracies, rhetors, passions, slanders
rise and fall with vanity and love, bind
moods to us: cranes, Li Po's moon, Panders'
promises of quick-won love, dry wine,
a passing joke, a pain, a sleepless dawn.
Every dog-eared page with day's decline
grants grace, a stay, dwelt in, long lingered on.
A delicate and feisty Keats, wild Blake
angle a glance and glare at him who'd miss the angry *how*
of things: the magic, prayer, the haunted grave.
Brash Byron despoils convention in his wake,
while Milton's stately ghost lifts furrowed brow,
and Shakespeare's spirit crashes like a wave.

Top Shelf

Skip quickly past the cavern of Charon
and break the clasp of self-created chains,
then wake me to the soft and fragrant rains
where ripe fields, steep vales, bright rivers run,
till all self-doubt, mistrust, and fear have gone.
Wash my eyes with visions, that I may see
white light, without which hues can never be.
May all survive the darkness when day's done.
        I were bold without my selfish doubt
        that tells me I can never see the stars,
        or touch the night, or hear the harmony
        of human love. Bound, within, without,
        such fears fetter me, behind the bars
        that would so shackle me from seeing me.

Early Studies

Old, mis-stressed eyes burn: something like the sun
inhabits deep inside them, makes them run
from thought to thought, script to script, find flavor
in dull stones and ancient knots few moderns savor.
Parchment fades. A skull's a lonely cheek.
But find the code, and dead words chant or speak,
sometimes. Dust uncovers insubstantial fruit;
the harsh shawm drowns out the gentle lute.
But simmered thoughts taste better if you share
them, and even bristling arguments can please
when sweet concord follows: an answer
that lasts, at least, a time. To quit, to spare
yourself some truth, means rest, whatever ease
one finds, has fled. To know: thought's chef; soul's dancer.

Reading Ovid

Remake me into music Muse, if you
be Muse indeed. With me as music, then,
amuse all those who see or hear, too.
Blood and foolery, all good and ill that, when
we break the seal, rush out in cataracts.
Plots as tight as seeds in the pod: the men
and women whose passion and excess refracts
our vision of the world; the fear and yen,
in equal mix, that echo in that Warning
Voice; the perfect word that finds but once
its perfect place; the whirling tune, adorning
all, that hides below, then spouts; the nonce
of light and shadow—in all, evolved, they play
live masques that strafe alike midnight, noonday.

Cato

Demosthenes harangued the roaring sea;
Aurelius Antoninus sought to grasp
what lies beyond the pomp of state, to key
his mind, to calm a vain heart, to clasp
the right hand of Zeno, knowing strength
and duty, courage come from will. Detach,
that comes first, as Krishna taught, the length
of the wide world away. Bring under latch
and lock the wild horses of desire. Know
the liberation of good work, of form,
of study, preparation, self-control.
Where Cato waits at the mountain shore grow
rushes: you must, when you arrive, conform,
and tie one round your waist. On the waves roll!

Augustine's Prayer

Purify, my God, my heart with fire.
Strike, tune, score it in a key
as harsh and human as Gethsemane.
Let cauterizing flame anoint, inspire.
Enkindle with your burning music, Lord,
a blazing, sword-broad passage to the soul;
infuse me with the notes of sweet accord,
glowing steady as a fresh fire's coal.
> You have seared the soul's flesh into dust;
> I have scorned youth's failing, brazen wail;
> I have known heart's tympani's despair.
> You have burned my discord into trust.
> Strike now a higher note than trumpet's hail:
> grace now this song of praise, this flame of prayer.

Alfred's Preface to Gregory's Pastoral Care

(rendered in sonnet form)

This errand brought stout Augustine
out of the south, over the salt sea
to Britain's island-dwellers, just as beforehand
the words were dictated by the Lord's ward,
bright-minded Gregory, Bishop of Rome.
That Pope pored over many pious speeches,
wrought in his wise heart a hoard of homilies,
that he among the righteous, most learned of Romans,
richest of spirit, most renowned for glories,
might turn the brave heathens to Heaven's host.
Reigning long after, King Alfred rendered
each blessed word into burnished English,
sent faithful scribes both north and south
to lighten the load of those who least knew Latin.

Duke William's Doomsday

"Conqueror," the French call him; the "Bastard," say
the English. One brave minstrel sings,
wrote Wace, Roland's Romance on the grey
eve of the English fall at Hastings.
With Harold dead, an arrow through his eye,
and none else strong enough to stop
the harry, William wins the throne, defy
who will. He'd establish, till he'd drop
from his horse at Mantes, Norman keeps,
strong shires, the Domesday Book. He burnt the North
to ash in vengeance as far as Tees leaps
its banks. The Danes and Scotsmen scurried forth
beyond his reach: peace is brief. His French
bent English with a strict, Latin wrench.

Ragnar Loðbrók's Death-Song

The Aesir will welcome me. Nor will I grieve
death—no point in that. It comes,
and I desire it. Ready, I leave,
since home the she-guards bid me. The thrum
of blood in my veins does not diminish.
Here from the Host-Leader's Hall Oðin
sent his daughters, shield-maids, to finish
the job. Gladly will I drink ale, O, then,
All-father, at the high-seat with the gods!
Life's allotted time, so short, has passed;
the sky shall bear my smoke, earth's sods
my footprint. As always I fight to the last.
Solve this, English king: O how the piggies
would squeal if they saw the old boar now!

Petrarca

Laura, I never knew her. Climbing Mount
Ventoux: now that had meaning. Didn't matter
who stood first upon the summit. The clatter
and bald bluster of law school, that fount
of litigation and irascible men, did not
fit me. In Avignon we tried to find
the Holy, escaped to Venice to unbind
ourselves from plague. A plague upon the lot:
all kept me from my poetry, my love,
from *Africa* to *Rime Sparse*. The Muse,
she has a loveliness beyond the reach
of men—as Laura has. *Post mortem*, shove
the law books in the sea, and set a fuse
to the unbeautiful. Learn, write, teach.

Dante to His Son, Overheard: Ravenna, 1321

"…nor Venice with its spices and its silk.
No question of returning home, but Home.
Beneath Sienna's walls with curdled milk
and crumbled figs far likelier than Rome,
then, how to stomach it? Worse yet,
no more to please, but simply to endure
until the final call. Yet nothing's set:
even to myself a self obscure.
Finitat, He said, and I dare not—
sacred words, and who'd bespeak what's done?
What can one poor exile do, my son?
A bit more stale bread? The wine I got
among the Bolognese—empty. Purge
my epic, as you feel the need or urge."

Palamon and Arcite Outside the Gate of Thebes

"As we two take the field today among
the teeming soldiers, swords a-gleam,
where soon our horses, tangled in the dung
and mangled fallen, heave us in the stream
of blood-washed toil, now let us pledge
our faith one final time, and blood be judge—
we more than cousins, more than brothers: *friends*
—that nothing part us till our mutual end."

      "For my part I would say the same, and add:
let him who first betray the other drown
in his own blood; let him who fail the other
never keep his love a day. I'm glad
to say, Old Friend, for peace and for renown
we fight, together always, Cousin, Brother."

One Miltonic Devil to Another

"If you are he—but oh, how fallen!"
Now I call you lost: only to break
silence. Tossed in Chaos' winds, like pollen
caught in a dust devil, they whirl, the crake
of solid bodies barely known, chained
by the darkness, to be changed again by the light of day.
The eyes will never adjust, rearranged
by what they've lost and yet remember, the flay
and scorch of memory of the Most High. Calm
they can never know again. Once the Thunder
comes, self-affliction reigns: they find no balm
in strength, such pain as makes the toes curl under.
"United thoughts… to bow and sue for grace,
Impossible!" Calamity begs only saving face.

Austen's City Limits

Hers is no country for old men.
Darcys always find a place, and Bingleys,
but a Mr. Bennett, like an old wen,
recedes. Dowagers, in pairs or singly,
wield most power, for they most surely
set the laws of who weds whom and judge
propriety and fortunes. Hers, most purely,
the realm of titles and estates that nudge
uncertain, sprightly girls to love, proclaiming,
theirs or others', when they're finally ready;
hers the girl of mind and heart, reclaiming
for her family some lost dignity: steady
of soul, if short in wealth… All's well: they marry on,
then show their husbands off like gold or carrion.

Byron Loved

the Greeks, and Vergil, Masaccio and Giotto,
and loved his sister more than a man ought to.
He won fame as a voice of generations,
inspiring youths' unseemly venerations.
Admiring ancient heroes, friend and foe,
he died for Greece, so far from home. Although
a club-foot kept his sporting life truncated,
he swam across the Hellespont buck naked.
Nabobs, ignoring prophets, clergy, seers,
appointed him among the House of Peers.
They threatened, when they'd finished his *Don Juan*,
To rip him—due respect to rank—a new one.
He gobbled oysters, mussels—steamed—and quohogs,
prepared thereby to write new randy prologues.
They filled his tomb with crystal balls and oujies,
and hired monks to clean his stone with squeegees.

Returning to Keats Returning to Lear

He lives in a world of October leaves
cacophonous with color, soon carpeted in snow.
Fresh pens dash among the stacked sheaves,
as the last hints of sun fade in the glow
of oil lamps too soon extinguished.
Youths still turn pale at a Keats ode
for love of vibrancy early extinguished.
The weight of the world, the slippery, cumbersome load
of creating clings too nearly. The clock
strikes, the hammer falls, lungs collapse;
regardless of time, the boat leaves the dock
early; swallows fly; diseases relapse.
But we rise from the cold with each re-reading
to find a fresh stanch for our wounds' bleeding.

On First, Looking Into Chapmen's Homer

Oft have I traveled on the basepaths, roamed
with many a single, double, stolen base,
round second, third, and sliding into home:
which efforts scribes and partisans embrace.
With diving catch and peerless throw, to come
at last into the Show and hope to grasp
a pennant wild, but never picked the plum
of grand October's Series, till a-gasp:
upon a seventh game, down by a run,
on first I stood—two outs, I had to hold—
in inning nine. Through rays of setting sun,
then, I saw Chapmen swing out, strong and bold,
looked on with cheering thousands, awed and tense,
as Chapmen's homer fell beyond the fence!

The Woman's Answer to Her Late Poet

By a feeble fire, with a half-read book,
I trust the fading words now. The eyes
barely see them, though they cross the page, look
for something new that isn't there. Sighs
spill yet from between those covers that buffer
memories too old and taut to forget.
Subjects, like the poets who treat them, suffer
loneliness and loss: poets seldom get
that far in their musings, lost in themselves
—a selfish art, that. In your *Byzantium*
you barely think of love: it swims, it delves,
it flies, and yearns for what has past, may come.
All is past or passing, posh or pith.
You didn't ask, just turned me into Myth.

Post-war Lost & Found

Alms, compassion, self-control: echo
of a Waste-World, whittled by war and flu
to dry sticks by shrapnel, when at last we knew
how to kill by scores. Cubism, Art Deco,
ExPressIonIsm made sense of gas and limb
sur-really fragged and browned to blitz: they
showed the beast required no jungle. "Pray,"
said the voice, abstain in public, stay in trim:
the respite's brief. Find solace in a glove,
in sport, in soup, in dust, in all the great
Globe possess; fear the dollar, states,
Commies, tyrants, foreign food, but love
your folks, your heroes, girls next door.
Blink, and get your chin up off the floor.

Room of Her Own

Surface tensions that make the Venus Flytrap
close; teeth that tear, claws that catch
the unwary Modern: worlds change, latch
the door that led away. The *puck* and *flap*
of tents at festivals remind: the rap
of winds on oily panes; the flimsy patch
that covers wounds; the rain-drenched match
that fails to light a lamp—each one a trap,
each one neglects its promise. Go then, at last,
to the Lighthouse with Dad, catch Septimus
before he falls, buy gloves, before the past
catch up. Avoid Despair: He'll laugh, and you'll fizz.
Who's afraid of Virginia Woolf? Virginia Woolf is.

Fire, Ice, and Light

Some say the universe began with fire,
while some insist it must have come from Light.
From what I know of smoldering desire,
either idea's allegorical, but slight:
to pare, as if it were a small thing, Creation,
given infinite variety and age,
down to a single source and immolation—
each Alpha needs Omega, says the Sage.
Ice must follow fire or light betimes.
But since we must remain direct and terse,
says Occam, and reason free of hope or ire
our stretched, old, dappled Universe:
fire dies in ashes; ice melts in rimes.
Light may, however, linger and inspire.

Hobbiton

When liquid light breaks over the hills' hoar-
frost, and night's thatch dissolves in gold,
milk bottles clink at the smial door,
and butchers, open before dawn, have sold
the day's first rashers, warm bread-smell
wafts through windows, wakes little ones
who dream of seed-cakes and scones. Dwell
with me awhile in this green land, where runs
and rills and tilled fields gleam like gems.
Well-fed folk sing their way
to work, knowing nothing of what evil stems
from orc-mines, steel forges, dray-
drawn slave-carts. Sauron's horsemen ride,
and hobbit hearts (ours) find no way to hide.

Gwendolyn Brooks

Born, Topeka, Kansas, raised in Illinois,
from Annie Allen, Bronzeville, and Hyde Park
she took experience, kindness, anger, poise,
and understanding, bent tradition to the quark
of Modern problems: racial hatred, greed,
poverty, exclusion, disdain for others' pain.
She found reserves of gentle irony, the seed
of personal and public voice. The grain
she saved in words, the chaff discarded. That voice
made magic with its alto sax: it dived
and soared. Through form, line, word, free choice,
alive amid the should'ring crowd, it thrived.
She won at last the world's veneration:
truest spirit, best of her generation.

At the Library Door

These hills and valleys have but gentle sways:
gentle the landscape of the reader's days.
We touch the heavens—high stars not too high—
rest free of lands where wearied worries lie.
Small rains pipe lightly as a flute,
and droplets cling along the leaves like fruit;
inside, we may imbibe the loves and losses
of the ancients, their joys, their pains, and sacred glosses.
A coat of mail, perhaps a coat of paint:
we can admire their passion or restraint
and live betimes among the saved or lost
for hours on end at no to little cost.
Come cold or hot, or technocrat elitist,
the book remains, *per* Horace, useful, sweetest.

BOOK OF DAYS AND NIGHTS

(for the cruelest month)

1. Vergil, The Aeneid, Book 1, lines 1-11

Of arms and a man I sing, who first from Troy's coast,
to Italy, driven by fate, came to Lavinian shores,
tossed over sea and land by the High Ones,
from savage Juno's memorable wrath.
Many his sufferings in the steps of war, till he raised a city,
brought his gods into Latium, whence come the Latin folk,
the Alban fathers, and the high ramparts of Rome.

Muse, remind me the cause, how that Divinity was angered,
why grieved, the Queen of the gods, so she wrought such troubles
that a man remarkable for virtue must endure all labors.
Can such wrath come from celestial spirits?

Of pen and Rome's poet I sing: may each line,
like his, speak piety, make life better, braver,
each poem find its proper beginning.

2. Evangelist

He sits on a bench where he wakes
by the Guadalupe, deeply sings
sermons to the ducks, slakes
noonday heat with a round-brimmed hat, flings
crumbs to the crows, interprets dreams,
smokes Camels in the hat's shade
as the brute sun steams
the sky green as jade.

He strolls on sere grass by the path
by the Guadalupe, waves
at the passing children without looking,
pities locusts that bake in the wrath
of the sun, cooking
brown as the grass,
as the Latins, the gringos, the slaves
who have toiled, as those who now pass
browning in the sun, in the sun.

3. Tools: A Sound Poem

Shrill drill bits dig slits.
Pincer-pliers catch, clip.
Spades thud, spread stones, notch roots.
Adze rips shreds.
Sledge wrecks rocks.
Wedge splits stacks.
Hammers knock, fix bent caps;
ball peen taps tops, rings pans right.
Claws rip spikes.
Wrench squeaks pipes, turns cranks.
Torch sears planks,
solders joints.
Sharp saw: locks nixed,
splits beams with sparks,
spits scree and sizzle.
Hatchets swipe, slice, pound.
All's fixed.

4. Arjuna on the Brink of Battle

Over Kuru's battle plain
the mad harmony of challenges and spears
rushes in a Shivan torrent.
Wheezy dust clouds tumble like fog off the Ganges,
covering my dead, the enemy's, alike.

The heat of the charge lightens me.
My heart swells, and last night's visions recede.
Pandu horses two-step over fallen bodies,
but the parched air mouths for their sweat and blood.
I do what I have always done.

I am a soldier as I am a man.
I am war, my nation, my enemy, someone's *karma*.
I heft my spear to pierce another nameless heart
untroubled in another dying breast.
I try to forget that I have talked with God.

The sky: an unremarkable blue.
I have eaten my bread and honey.
In the stench of bodies and the throatless heat,
who would know what love galls me,
what dreams trouble a young man's sleep?

5. An Art and Science of Stone

Woodhenge: to imagine it breakable
defies sense and desire. *Stone*
means "permanent," beyond the acheable,
chilling sense of loss that bone
redounds as pain, separation.
Height, weight wring intimidation.

Yet for all the dustless, tumbled
dolmans, something close and homey:
air filled with rain, rumbled
over the silver-green loamy
plain—it takes a mind in disarray
and lends persistence. To do, to say,

to *make*. Making lingers, *means*,
adds walls, howes, paths,
though chalk in time turns green,
and magnitude whips wind to wrath.
In the distance Salisbury spire
recalls the ghosts, makes blood of mire.

6. Catullus, Carmen 86
(Carmina Ottanta-sei), ca. 60 B.C.

(a translation)

Quintia, "So shapely!" say the many. For me, too,
so white, so tall, so straight she stands! And I confess
the glories of these qualities, each alone.
But I deny that's beauty: no charm, no grain
of grace dwells in so great a body. Lesbia,
there's a total beauty: she has stolen Venus' glories.
Every one!

7. Healing Equi-nocks

Bent-kneed winter weather
poised
for its final pleasure
fields
a bowl of sun
and lea

ps:

for a lick of Spring.

8. Everything's Waiting for You

Starry Night lights
street-shores fjord-like—
Bridges' penumbral shadows
mug innocent widows
of waves of serpentine neon

wind windwind WIND
surfs a fluttery rush,
pinches hats, grinds,
cuts kisses in half

North to Wrigley, south to Comisky
where have you gone, Michael Jordan, O?
A love-glance twists to a filament.
A dog, waiting for a pet, gets frisky.
An old priest tugs at his cassock,
rubs in liniment.

9. Skyway

south on the Dan Ryan 70 74 67 42 18 ! !! 0 0 0 0
move right right RIGHT! You Bastard…
Swinging onto the Skyway
off the Damn Ryan, thank you
two lane, one lane, oh no
McDonalds?
Bridge ahead!
sky
    way
        sky
            way
            Sky
            Way
        Don't
    look
down!
steady now… SPEED

steady
steady
steady

oh, the tar-brushed Gary air

the mills
the furnaces
the Dead
Inferno
dust smoke grit haze reflux smog acidy acridy greygreygrey

south to Merrillville
and the unremitting, unrepentant, unyielding flat of Indiana

10. News from the Burning Lake

(from Paradise Lost)

Such extraordinary gems here:
topaz, ruby, ~~chrysoberyl~~...

Surfing the fire-whelms,
Cascading, *acciaccatura* runs on the lyre—
What songs a whip can make
on a delicate back!

Teeming crowds, swarms,
esteemed in their time,
can hardly wait to get here—
O Sophists, forfend! Ha ha.

Each day new ways of persiflage, badinage,
escalade, fusillade.
No calamity so great
as amity.

One thing never changes:
those baleful, baleful eyes.

11. After the Metamorphoses

Remake me into music, Muse,
if you be muse indeed;
amuse with me as music
all who hear, see, and bleed.

Assume me music, make good use,
then make me man again
to linger as your notes induce
in all that eases pain.

Bring skilled notes of such constancy,
that I may sing you, sing me,
and never from view
lose me, lose you.

12. Entering the Interim

Bruce and Hugh cleaned dog poo
while the poodle fiddled with riddles.
Oodles of coddled toddlers
scooped noodles from griddles
as two foodies canoodled,
two biddies tittered over the poodles' piddles,
and six mottled models doodled with swizzle sticks.
Better peen, keen, croon, and shoo
than fritter caboodles stuck in the middle.
A few dizzy tutors twitter "toodle-loo."

13. Warm-up for Aretha Franklin

(in honor of the singer, Langston Hughes, and John Dryden)

Slowly, dulce, in hazy light.

Then, pronto:

tintinab, tintinab, tintinab, tintinab—
Queen's a-comin'…
Now: Ready!

Cornets and flugelhorns, French horns and sousaphones:
       God save the Queen!

Drum, drum, drum
drumdrumdrum
     drum, drum
        drumdrumdrum

Strings, swing, wing,
     sing like angels for peace,
        sorrowful, serious, tense now, RELEASE!

Clarinet, smooth as milk
     Saxophone, cool and aloof
     Now the flute, sweet as silk
     Base guitar lowers the roof

Joyful keyboard, flash and dance,
     fingers fugue in a tuneful trance

But my, my, my! what that voice can do,
turning you, and me and you,

into harmless musical goo—
riff, run, rant, rumble,
purge my deroticized mumbled jumble.
Remake me with your music, Aretha,
Improved, true, and *new*.

14. Tuan McCairell to St. Finnian

…all dead, you know: disease had got them.
I survived: the old gods, I thought,
had kept me, perhaps to suffer pain and sorrow.
Now you break in upon my solitude:
you believe, I know, you have my good at heart,
so I will tell you what I can recall.
A vision first I thought it, fever's dream.
As I slept off the swell of June sun's madness,
I, Partholan's nephew, from old Noah,
chosen to survive the pestilence, worn,
crawled through the wastes, pursued by wolves, leapt up
a stag, to flee: my shape had changed, I knew
not how. Horrific nights: to hear their howls.
As king of deer I wandered knotty crags,
the overhanging woods and slippery creeks.
But then in time I longed to fight the wolf
I'd fled, and fell into a dream again.
Even the stag dreams, or so I thought.
But then in dream I felt the change again,
again, like Adam, woke to find my dreaming
true. I rose not as before, so high,
but stronger, equal to the wolf, and mean,
though not in station: chief of boars, to sniff
and grunt amidst the brush, a king of brutes.
I tell you truly, to have such power jolts
the heart so full of life, that you can tear
warm flesh from bone with fangs
a finger long and fine as iron dirks.
Time came I tired of root and rut,
and with my eyes my thoughts rose up:
the birds, light of bone and wing, called.
My heart answered when sleep grasped,

and up I flew, an eagle, treading wind,
balanced high above both cliff and shore,
and fed on cats and coneys, king of air,
not one claw less the royal than before.
To soar, to dive faster than a knife:
great pleasure there, I must admit. But flap
or scream, the change came on again betimes,
and down I tumbled to the curling waves.
I would have fought that change, but ere a man
can draw a breath, I wriggled as from birth
the sea had shaped my course, and, king of salmon,
up the coursing river swam to spawn.
In the currents how the small fish dart,
atop the shallows how the dragon-flies
zag and burr in the sun!—a better life,
that, than you may think, so little there
to trouble little mind, so blank of thought.
Thought perhaps had saved me the fisherman's
hook and net: O how I fought! and I'd
not wish a scaling and a roasting on any
creature, not the most ill-tempered beast
of all the lot. Fine meat I made for Cairell's
wife: I think they cooked me in brown butter
and fresh herbs. But something in my meat
the fire couldn't quiet. Whatever I am,
deep down, would not lie still: I crept
into her womb and lay content nine months.
Nature ever stirs, dear Christian father!
So I was born again. Cairell named
me *Tuan*. I grew again into a man,
awoke to thought, again a king, ha!
Another dream? Old I've grown, and all
the folk I've known have gone. I know the tear
of savage rocks on soft soles, the leather
of the working palm, the beard soaked in sweat
and mud better than the soft pillow, the warm
embrace of love, or the hot meal on a winter's
night. As man and beast I've learned to grunt
and curse and gulp rough food whenever,

wherever I can claw it from the earth.
This cabin has its comforts. I have lived
here long, an age perhaps, content with time
alone. I tell my tale to the passing wind,
or now and then a storm-lost guest.
These transformations: dream or prophecy,
you of all may best determine. None
I knew remains alive; I haven't heart
to write, and knobby finger-joints refuse
the job. Salt waves cleanse them, when I
can walk that far, and I have grown too old
for tears. The sun beats gently on my shrinking
world; skies cloud; rain falls; yet I remain
a savage and a king. Despite the lure
of sleep, I thirst, I hunger, and I dream.
Hope sinks daily with the evening sun,
till now you raise it once again: a final
time? One more rebirth for aged Tuan
you promise, with a sprinkle of your holy
water, a pot of incense, and a prayer?
One god has proven victor at the last?
Open then your book and read, or tell
all as you please. I have rendered up
my tale. I will listen now.

15. Unemployment Line

hire oh, hire oh
glyphs pinched in old Want Ads
Hieronimo's hired again, ha ha
Crossword's done—now for Sudoku
graphing interviews: North Side, Mich. Ave., burbs West
cough COUGH—shitty cold
online, in line, feline
queue, cue—que?
AT&T, IBM, AIG, PhD, AIDS
Gary, Republic, Big Shoulders, bad knees
Before the crash, before the Fall, BEFORE
Can you see in the dawn's surly light? At least the Cubs won
scuffing, scuffing, mark the floor—MARK it!
lost, lost: can't come back tomorrow
tomorrow and tomorrow and in… creeps… a walking
shadow

16. Akhenaten

"Look on my Works, ye Mighty, and despair!" —Shelley

I Horemheb, Horus, Pharoah,
god, guardian of the people's present and past,
do so inscribe the removal by force, necessity, and decree
of all images, passages, and works
of the false A—, predecessor, heretic.
His legacy will not survive my reign.

We, the glory of Egypt,
would have the old ways,
would wipe away the scourge of all change,
of all will but our own will,
all lies and their makers.

Our servants have defaced the sarcophagus,
scoured the stones,
made papyrus into palimpsest.
The sand will swallow all
in its endless sleep.
Sand covers all,
and Death decrees what even I cannot.

Not only death.
The Nile takes all things,
or Ra,
or the flies,
or simply time,
to which I, Horemheb Horus Osiris,
only I
in my glory
am immune.

But not, in the quiet of the night, my memory.
"Egypt, Nubia, Syria, each in its place
and all things hidden from the human face:
so did you, Aten, settle on the tongue
all creatures' names, rung by rung,
their fates from the body's dawn,
substance and shadow to me drawn...."

His words in my thoughts, too, I will wipe clean. I *will*.

17. Detainee

At the time,
knowing nothing: where am I? why am I here?
I heard someone say *Guantanamo*—
maybe a name, a place. I don't know where.
Hooded, I spent hours, my first time in a plane.
When we landed, I wanted only a glimpse of the sea.
A whiff, an echo of breakers,
something to stanch the monotonous horror
of feverish bodies,
of parched tongues,
of the cloying threats and blows—
a word, a sigh from family would have done.

A new king has come, no *imam*, they say,
more committed than the last to the wellspring
of brine waiting in the human heart,
the sour scathe that draws the skin off the body.
Stretched on my belly,
I peer beneath the tarp that covers my cell.
Guards come again with tubs and wires.
I think of my family in the desert at sunset.

One of the guards, for amusement, I think,
quotes to me from their sacred scripts.
Parts I try to remember, one that says,
"So government of the workers
by the rich, and for the rich,
shall not perish from this earth."
I may not have got it right.

18. Yates Said

"I think it better that in times like these
a poet remain silent"—safe, deft of him.

But should we rather hear politicos
in their bombast
               bullets,
                             bayonets—their bilging roils,
pundits incessant in their constant quarrels?

Must the singer purse her lips,
the scientist turn corporate in retreat,
the painter shred her canvas,
the dancer squat flat on his feet?

Have we nothing left
but the pixilated bluster of a tweet?

19. Mad King George

repeated himself, repeated himself,
yet old Farmer George put Boney on the shelf.
Whigs denounced him; Yankees hated him,
but almost no one intimidated him.

To punish his enemy's contumacy
turned out but a part of his lunacy,
yet he let all that tumble into the past,
saw a friend in rebellious foes at last.

Foaming at the mouth, he withdrew to Kew,
kept the prosperity of Britain in view,
no longer a wronger of *dei imago*,
Mameluke, rakehell, lion, mago.

In his time a symbol of war and schism,
the face of English imperialism,
assumed by his time porphyric or insane,
he learned at last not to rule, but to reign.

Now he's back from afar with a new avatar,
ready to rack and to bomb and to tar,
a bird on the wing with insults to fling,
immune to knowledge and wisdom, this king.

An ego wakened with inheritance's loom,
like a child from the womb, a ghost from the tomb,
in a world more techy than way back then,
he'll rise to unbuild it again.

20. Drawing, Awaiting Color

Taloned night, shadow-heavy,
tugs at earth's hem,
circles seamed earth
for a moaned requiem.

In mauve lamplight, canvas night
through shriven mists cradles
the moon like an egg,
while the stars dip their ladles.

Crossed clouds spread
first-fluttered wings, crave
sun stirring from down under—
till pent morning brushes in its wave.

21. Same Time, Same Place

Cockeyed hands park at two o'clock.
Fifties jukebox doesn't work,
so I hum "Route 66" with the tube.
Eisenhower on the half-shell
stares from a bloodless tip,
and the last swig of lager
goes down to a twinge of nausea.
Over the ranks of bottles
a red light pulses in the mirror,
round and quivering as a pouting lip.
Strained eyes stray
into the laughter-bludgeoned glass,
and time limps past the sprained clock.
Twenty years and we
do the same dive
swill the same beer
tell the same jokes
and the dislocated night gasps like death.

22. Dido, to Herself

Even here he comes, speaks in that voice,
here, where men must not come, where the dead,
having flexed what existential choice
Nature lent them, must go where they're led.

Gods love a hero, whether they admit it or not.
There, for one noon, one we lay on our stony bed
outside my city, which Rome will reduce to rot.
He may speak till Doomsday. I will turn my head.

23. Battle Plain

Generals like a gymnosperm
bounce hoplites, quincunxed,
whose lavaliere spears
tock like glockenspiels.

Post prostaglandins, blood pints
fulminating, propinquity
brings, for the living,
bongs, songs, and scuppernong.

24. Blocks

concrete   but   fragile
slabs   put together   walls that end—
alone   they make   nothing
won't serve   substantial   ends—greed
the general   blockishness   it continues
purposes   serve   the purposelessness

25. Cuchulain Meets the Washer at the Ford

Not Emer's entreaties, nor Dectera's bloody cup
could turn him, not all the world, nor for stubbornness,
but because he knew what was to come, what *must*.

At the ford he saw the Washer scrubbing, scrubbing
his shield, heard her wailing, thus
his fate confirmed. She turned, wide-eyed, and spoke:

"Take one last glance, hero, over the plain
of Emania, home to heart and victories.
Hear my death song: your death song."

"Long ago at one far-distant ford,
before some long-forgotten war I can't
myself remember, where father, husband, son
lay food for ravens on the field, I found
and washed their bloody shields, and begged
the gods for their return, and cursed the gods
who draped the battle plain with blood,
with blood of my blood.
Once happy I, my fiery hair danced
in the wind, my wild screams rose to the clouds.
When the sky cracked, I crumbled in the rain,
vowed deathless to the deathless gods to cry.
And so those faithless gods have left me here
to weep for every hero whose body lies,
or whose body soon will lie,
opened to the eagle and the oozy sun,
each warrior subject to a tyrant creed
as I am bound to hate for wasted blood.

Far greater enemy than Maev or Lewy
waits ahead, Cuchulain: faceless, empty—
and yet you have the joy to die. For me,
who cannot die, who, what remains?
What comfort, Cuchulain, can you offer?
Will you shed a tear for me?

Her wailing passed into the sky like smoke.
The image faded, the raging water eased and fled.
The hero shook the rains and trotted on.

26. Breakfast

"Uncle Portnoy will hate his porridge," the blackbird said.
"He should," Aunt Griselda snipped, "having eaten that quince."
"I find pomegranates delicious," said the baby, sighing.
"We've never had them here, not ever," the Shar Pei insisted.
Little Winkle spat, and spat, and spat his milk.
"Someone must clean those filthy colanders," Grandmother moaned.

Badger, listening by the window,
shook his head and decided to go out for lunch.

27. Belfry

From morning's mandolin-string wind
birds reverberate like quick-plucked notes,
cling to windy eaves, tangled in currents,
wring like the sound of rain.
At a gust like the cymbal of footsteps,
they burst into the sky like a bomb.

But in the cool twilight, when dreams
pass like a whisper in the ear,
a soft-tongued bell minor-keys
"Come Thou Font of": lucid notes beacon
through mist-cathedralled streets
to soothe the soul like a balm.

28. Crossing the Bridge

1

The river has its own seasons, regardless of calendars.
From the middle of the bridge you can see them all
as they shape the water to their own ends.
I cross the bridge daily to keep an eye on the water:
someone must....

In earliest spring, as the day begins to stretch its light,
the last perplexed rays cast demon eyes on the water.
High with unseasonal rain, the river, in a vast shadow,
rises, meets the eye with obsidian,
and sunset casts clouds overtop in orange and blue.
Eliot's fog skitters over the water and its clouds,
making depth impossible.

2

When air and water finally warm with summer,
the surface oblates a layer of green algae.
Thin and oily, it fractals its own course,
ignoring the water beneath.
A goose, too slow in rising,
squawks as it nearly crashes into the bridge,
aborts its course, and sinks again, unhappily,
onto the ooze.

3

In autumn pigeons, testing their flocks,
fling themselves like fisherman's nets
over the water that rushes to the dam beyond the bridge.
They drop, twist, rise again above the bridge,
empty of everything but resiliency.

4

Winter, before it can scratch the water into ice,
turns it black: thick as coal tar,
it moves as though the bridge has squeezed it
from a large-mouthed bellows. Oh black water–
soon months of stillness will hold it
creaking, yellow-white with streaks of false, blue youth.

The bridge is its own place, and can,
through us and its waters,
make a heaven of its hell, a hell of its heaven.

29. Reasons for Golf

Eighteen days in Middle-earth—
perch, dale, bank, wet! oh, god…
All too soon the turf thy tower,
the game preserves something dearth-
of-days can't soil, and thick sod
cushions, whether spirit soar or sour.
Nae wind, nae rain, sky blue
As a robin's egg. For beach, copse,
grass green as a dragon's wild eyes—
at once congenial, mythic, calm: the hue
of the day rules, and each tomorrow chops
wedges from new rough, emits fresh sighs.
But here's the thing: all else sharp and dark
as too young, peaty Scotch, the Swiss clock-
perfect strike of club on ball unbinds
a smooth-as-a-windmill steady hark-
ening to perfection instantaneous. Ship from dock
launched in eagle-splendor seeks, *finds*.

30. Trains

(for Bev)

Can you remember
youthful spring mornings,
waking to the cries of new-hatched birds,
bathing in the bubbling air
when we ran gold in the sun?

Can you remember
the train's perspicuous welcome,
greeting the still towns
across the plains
or below Appalachian
hills bunched along the river
on tracks stretched like taffy
as far as we could see?
How the children danced like robins
on spruce- and maple-lined lawns,
how the morning sounds
of milk bottles delivered,
trash collection by thin, gloved men,
coffee percolating,
the root-beer smell of sassafras tea,
and the year's last school-bus cries
when we ran to school
with a ball and a glove and book or two?

Can you remember strolling, youthful summer days
when the round sun
pressed down like a palm,
steadily, evenly,
and sweat streamed from your brow

as you turned double plays
or raced in the woods of oak and hickory,
the cool green creek bed
and butterflies spiraled on gusts?

Can you remember
how September rains rang like cymbals
on the metal patio porch,
and you ran in among the long drops
from the fragrant, half-cut cherry logs
split and stacked for winter's fires?
On fall mornings aching with apples
how the old black Chevy wouldn't start
when the maples dripped dew in the fog,
the rust we tried to coax from the bumper?
How the freight trains
and the passenger trains
sounded daylight's shadows,
come from far, going far
as the vermillion-spilled skies
and moonlit copse and corners,
how the engine belched a groan,
a hoarse laugh, a greeting
under the back-yard peach tree,
the oaks, the birch along the river,
the dangling willows like bangs
under hair brushes?

Can you remember
metronomic percussions of the endless trains,
cars beyond our count
in the dank autumn nights
or kicking up the dusty smell
of dying leaves in pre-snow November,
silhouettes of Friday-night football crowds,
fathers cheering son's glories
in the season's last games,
another year freed of its many stories,
when the railroad tracks

smelled of cold creosote,
and the night sky bowed
to meet the rails
where the hills broke in the west
and the plains opened up
into brushstroke clouds
unravelling as the wind blew the stars
into fireflies,
when ghosts of the old passenger trains
carried soldiers, so many, toward war,
and some few back home again?

Oh, can you remember
that bleak Midwestern sky
when October's first rime
rolled over the billiard-table farms
and the whistling sparrows
fizzled like a wet match
with December's ice ponds,
the last leaves clinging
to the hickories and the buckeyes and the sycamores,
the last sere leaves clinging like icicles
then buried under the snows
that nipped the lungs of winter?
How December crept in, the rustle
of her icy feet echoing in leafless boughs
as the geese left behind the year's last calls
from a sky swept clean of clouds?
How trains, more insistent,
wailed in the night,
the rush of the clanking tank cars,
the shock and jar of the freight cars,
rank upon rank of coal cars,
counting the shining oil cars
on and on and on
to the last clack of the dull red caboose,
ringing echoes under the domed sky?
And how the shrill whistle,

HOOT, howl, hoot hoot!
once, twice, three times,

sliced midnight's crystal-cold air
deep in snow-swept winter,
how we saw the prints in the snow
for the last time
of the old man,
the old switchman
we called by so many names
who stalked the sultry summer nights
and fall football nights
and frosty winter nights
and that last still, chill December night
when he stood knee-deep in drifts
to hear, up close,
the train's long, lonely, lovely call
once more, deep in his bones to hear it?
And how the steps trailed off
into the woods' tiny warmth
as the passing train's low moan
flooded the night air with its song
of all that's past, of loss, lamentation, of death.
How he must have settled in the murky darkness
under the swirling snow
for that last, long night
to listen to the wind
sweeping like a falcon
before it, too, died away.
How the west wind calls
when even the stars sleep,
and thoughts, like the night,
when the wind dies down,
grow stone still.

Ah, can you remember, too,
the slow, slow passing of January,
of February like an ice-quilt,
till the sparrows chattered on a March morning,

and the wrens scattered from the rails,
flung themselves like paint flecks
into the pale sky
at the first hooting call of the morning train?
How the dawn-fed air crackled,
and spring breeze cooed,
and the lip-red sun
melted the last remnant snows
into slush puddles
smelling of leaf-decay and winter dust—
yet spring settled on the doughty trees,
buds like peach-fuzz glowing lime-like
from their tiny cocoons,
and sap rose from root to limb
to get closer to the sun,
to hear the old sounds,
to stretch and bristle
at the rattling baritone of train-song,
plaintive, lurking, longing, loving
promising:
how it swept like a whisk,

dislodged

a weak bud from a waking linden,
and we ran and we called
and we bounced along and over the tracks
from morning to night,
and late, late under the moon's eclipse
we would watch and listen
to its matins or lauds, when we felt so alive,
when broken light would hardly trouble sleep,
but crisp whistle calls
splattered morning's palate-riff
till the train long as summer
curled off beyond the hills
into cat-calico dawn
through every waking valley
from, and to, where the warm wind blows.

WOMEN OF MIDDLE-EARTH:

A Poem Sequence Based on the Works of J.R.R. Tolkien

1. Lúthien Tinúviel

The two-in-one I am, who won
my suit with Mandos: a death,
and so a mortal love. I'd done
what gods would not, or breach
free will, what men beneath the sun
could not for strength or reach,
in honor of queen Elbereth.

I felled the greatest Enemy with song.
Courage, day to day, before
and after deeds nor right nor wrong
endures the darkness, lights the will.
Two hands my Beren won, and one he lost
that grasped the fated Silmaril,
the stone that shone of Valinor.

This truth I learned, through all we've done:
Music and the heart are one.

2. Galadriel

Who has seen a star of Valinor
walks in its unforgiving gleam.
It burns each waking thought
like a living dream.

Eregion and Doriath and Lorien,
from the sweet, sad days of Feanor,
from Tol Sirion to my land of trees:
no memory fades of the Noldor.

We fought in the mountains, fought in the fields,
fought for the forests and the rills,
saved our world but never regained
the heaven-gleam of the Silmarils.

One a golden curl, one sweet earth,
one got foresight afar.
And I placed in one small, plump palm
a beam from a star.

3. Eowyn

My lord king, reborn to youthful might,
ordered me to miss the fight,
but my sword brought the Witch King
from undead darkness to burning night.

Our glory dimmed with sacrifice—
we lost so many proud, bold men,
we won the day we had to win
but lost who will not come again.

The grimmest among mortal men
I felled, with help of the smallest one.
I watched a girl's love crowned as king,
but found a woman's in a Steward's son.

4. Arwen Undómiel

Each fought in her own way:
some with sword, some with hope,
some with magic, some with love,
love born in an innocent glance
and deepened by the world's mischance.

Some sadness now, in fading light,
for what we had, and are, and know,
my elf-folk now depart these lands,
rejoicing in our Morning Star,
and naming me our Evenstar.

A girl among my folk, and yet
I've known a thousand years of war.
I've faced my danger, faced my joy:
undying love in the new King's sighs,
in a slowly dying Ranger's eyes.

Beyond each dream, beyond each thought
I knew love, know it still:
a son in mortal ashes caught.
My time as mother, daughter, wife:
in balance with this death, this life.

5. The Sorrows of Melian

Who knows
where grows
so lovely a garden
as Lórien?

Who knows
where sing
so prettily
the lómelindi?

They sing the loss
of Elwë/Thingol,
my elvish soul,
the seas across.
Forget. Forget.

Who sees
where flees
Galadriel,
so fair, so fell?

Who knows
where shows
now and again
the face of Lúthien?

Sing all Valar
and all Maiar
Two Trees that glow
to pierce my sorrow.
Forget. Forget.

6. The Entwives' Walking-Song

Whose fields these are I think I know, I do.
Their gorse and heather brush the hills with blue.
Lake winds whisk by and whistle in the rocks,
greet crooning thrush and hardy laveroks.

> Chorus:
>
> Turra-loma-lurra-lumba-lu,
>   among the valleys green and mountains blue.
> Turra-loma-lurra-lumba-lu,
>   tomorrow to fresh woods and pastures new.

Whose streams these are I think I know, I see.
When I step in, the trout and chubb will flee.
Night birds gale out some half-remembered songs
as minnows spiral in the billabongs.

Whose coombs these are I think I know, I feel.
Their cool and deep pools make my senses reel.
Fells drop to tors and then to quiet leas.
Their loams turn sand and open to the seas.

Whose moors these are I think I know, I'm sure.
The earth sheds peat and rapid streams run pure.
Slick cyclones lick the sea frets as they pass,
I brush them as my toes dig in the grass.

7. Halbarad's Song of Ulbandi

Fluithuin bore a son,
O sorrows of Middle-earth!
a son of pain, a son of fire,
Ulbandi, ogress, bore but one,
O suffering Middle-earth,
but one so dire!

Even Ogress must tarry
ere through the fiery fogs
her courage she gather:
could not even carry
the Lord of Balrogs
To Morgoth, his fell father.

Ulbandi, Ogress, mother,
Middle-earth-stone's daughter,
in world-wide-sorrow
could not bear another
such child of slaughter,
such a one to harrow.

Kosomot, of fiery hosts,
though she of stone,
would burn any earthen womb.
Before him all boasts
fell silent, with kin or alone.
He made of his mother a tomb.

8. Berúthiel

Mad Queen Berúthiel was no Tinúviel;
evils effluvial oozed from her thoughts;
she loathed her husband and all things connubial,
and most of all hated her cats.

All would fear and all would flee them,
All would curse who'd chance to see them:
One white cat with nine black brothers,
one to question and report on the others.

> Nine cats to watch them all,
> one more to berate them;
> ten cats to please her whim
> and one queen to hate them!

She measured the sun and timed the tides
watching the sea from Pelargir;
she traced the valleys of the glassy moon,
saw far, but wanted to see farther.

Her man loved to gaze at the silvery waves,
while she hid away in her wrath;
he kept to his throne and ignored her raves,
so she fled to Osigiliath.

For she hated those waves, hated Gondor,
saw life as a plague of disaster;
she deserted her home, for she hated her mate,
ill-choosing Turannon Felastur.

She devised a machine to turn men mean,
threw the switch to turn the power on;
had she half a chance, with one bitter glance
she'd have made herself into Sauron.

> The angry queen, the queen of mean,
> queen of cats and queen of hate,
> childless queen, queen of spies
> was exiled by her mate.

She sailed away far south of Umber,
tamed for servants a panther and a bear.
She spied on peoples and lands beyond number
and dwelt in the land of nightmare.

She preferred to the company of men and women
a host of loathsome toads and bats.
Her body, 'tis said, was consumed when dead
by a herd of feral cats.

> One queen to spy on them all,
> till nine familiars doomed her;
> seven lands to sigh with relief
> when the wild at last consumed her!

9. Finduilas

Cliffs: they draw us.
In part the sea, in part the gulls.
Mostly the drop, with nothing to stop us
from the whirlpool's culls.

Above Amroth keep bloom
white mariposa and the asphodel;
below, percussive waves swell
in their mutual tomb.

No sun fills Gondor's Shadow.
Names: they carry sorrow
half alive in fading yesterday,
not dead tomorrow.

Boromir, his father's son,
more honored, and publicly brave;
Faramir, his mother's son,
must tend our graves.

Oh, my dear son!
A mother's love must replace
a wife's for a husband,
a touch, a kiss, a face.

> *Each day a world of must.*
> *Few words of love, and fewer jests.*
> *In stone my memory rests,*
> *myself in dust.*

10. Tar-Míriel on the Face of Meneltarma

I, the jewel-daughter,
hardly party to this slaughter,
with no excuse of fate
a queen without a grave,
alone, washed clean of hate,
facing before the world comes to know of karma
this green, cold wave crash on Meneltarma.

From the water's well and hiss
forced to the edge of this rough abyss
as to the bed of that dead king,
I, now a loveless, nameless thing
lie swathed in fear.
How sweet it would have been
at least to have seen this end with Elantir.

Terror of the end-time enslaves us
once we know even the gods will not save us.

11. Rosie Cotton

I stood with Mother
and with Nibs and held another
pitch-fork of my own; I thought
the Men had come, and that I ought
to swing a weapon, like my brother.

When Sam appeared
outside the door I nearly cheered,
he looked so fine with mail and sword.
I teased that he should keep his word
and tend his master. In truth I feared

that once again I'd lose him.
We followed, Nibs and I, a-trim
in mind, our hearts afire
with Dad and Sam to save the Shire.
About time, too! Ready, grim.

12. Azogesh, Goblin Princess

Past the fight, unless I die,
I'll bake the elves up in a pie,
and for the men, those dirty snurks,
I'll chase them to the ground with dirks.

Before the ring of victory
beyond the caverns of the King,
the only light beneath the stars:
the shining of our scimitars!

Burn away their towns and towers,
Fill their lands with tunnels and shafts,
and where they dug our *mithril* and gold,
you'll only hear our shouts and laughs!

13. Ioreth, Wise-Woman of Gondor

The hands of a healer, says the medical lore.
We had no *athelas*, at least not in store.
In the butteries we found it, to freshen the air,
but dried leaves, though still clean and fair.

I have seen kingsfoil, by the garden wall.
Such hands as the King's, I have never seen:
palms so broad, fingers so long and lean.
It is good to be remembered, though for something small.

They called me "Flighty" when I was a child,
but I learned the herbs, the bones, the rheums.
I bore a daughter, so sweet and wild,
gave up my husband to a soldier's tomb.

"Men will remember your words," he said,
Wise Mithrandir. And good Faramir's pain fled.

14. Elbereth

A Elbereth Gilthoniel!
O Varda Elentári!
Shaper of Telperion's light,
Bless'd star-queen Tinwetári!

First daughter of Ilúvatar
sings earth to wake or rest;
of all that Eru sung or made:
wisest, brightest, best.

Glory of each Elven prayer,
midnight bright as noon;
stars like snowflakes compliment
her sun and waxing moon.

>Alone the Hobbit in Shelob's lair
>Alone the traveler on Caradhras
>Alone Arwen with Narsíl's shards
>Alone the Ranger in the Wastes
>Alone the Dwarf in exile's mines
>Alone the Ent in Fangorn's depths
>Alone—but not alone.

>Blessed by Lúthien in her song
>Blessed by Beren in his love
>Blessed by Idril in Eärendil
>Blessed by Elwë in Melian
>Blessed by Faramir in Eowyn
>Blessed by Gandalf in all labors
>Blessed—and ever blessed!

A Elbereth Gilthoniel!
O Varda Elentári!
Shaper of Telperion's light,
Bless'd star-queen Tinwetári!

15. Viðumavi and Valacar

Lo, we have heard how in homage-days
princes of Gondor, grand men and proud,
rode to Rhovanion's land-rich tribes,
ambassador-allies, armed but amiable,
to strengthen their ties, serve their treaties,
gladden the mead-halls: those were good men!
There lived a princess, prudent and lovely:
Vidumavi, maid of virtue,
wielder of wisdom in the woods of Wilderland.
Valacar, king's son, found first a companion,
like-minded leader in the noble lady.
He asked her a boon to assure their alliance,
that the lady would have him, husband to her heart.
With her father's permission she parted for Gondor,
joined her new mate, the jewel in his crown.
Guardian of the green lands for the greater good
married a guest-lord, yet felt love growing.
A new name they gave her, Galadwen of Gondor;
she gladly accepted to please both peoples.
Deep grew their love, yet not long her lifetime.
She left a son, strong in the courtyards,
Assailed by Kin-Strife, tested in conflict;
a mother's son made his legacy secure,
affirming a friendship the horsemen hallowed,
the White City's wisdom with Wilderland's courage,
for love of the lady, best of the northlands.

SENRYU SEQUENCE

1

Meeting at the coffee shop: there!
      August's sere lifting.
Colleague: waits at the door—Friend?

Brick façade, orange awnings:
      like Florentine roofs.
Greetings, Miltonist!

Inside: Vivaldi.
      Smell of veal, garlic, and mushrooms.
Baroque of lilies.

2

Table by the fountain!
      Altar-like, it pearls, whispers.
Ready to talk poems.

Sun through front windows.
      Tall waiter, immaculate.
Tomatoes, basil.

Student talks Milton.
      "Espresso, coffee, or tea?"
I winter in Dante.

3

Water, still and flowing.
        Menus turn in long fingers,
hand a roughed lily.

Dante's circling passions;
        Milton's arbor serene;
a cup falls—smashes.

Primo, limbic salad?
        then a crisp Frascati—
Then something broiled…

4

She: Caesar Salad?
        I: *bistecca* florentine?
Tusk and tussle.

Blue cheese dressing, yes?
        No, raspberry vinaigrette?
Wind jars the windows.

Mussels, *pasta fagiol*.
        Dusk: half moon rising white.
Pleasures of good talk

5

Espresso lightning.
        Fragrant tea for sipping—
Bergamot will-o-wisps.

Asparagus dip,
        olives, bread, *caprese*:
tongue toccatas.

Shakespeare's now in bloom.
        Dust of a Miltonic voice:
Paradise restrained.

6

Rereading's rewards:
        cheesecake with dark, tart cherries.
The fountain bubbles.

Joys not of knowing,
        but of learning more, finding.
Bite of the lemon.

Descend. Climb. Then…
        Strikes the postulent's shoulder.
Flock of birds rising.

7

Salad, meat, sweet.
        Glint from night-glazed windows:
Vergil from the *Comedy*.

Scent of flowers renews:
        Calla, Tiger, Lilies-of-the-valley—
first candle burns low.

She gazes into the lion's face.
        Musk and fruit of rich red wine:
black rose and leather.

8

What I want for you.
        Notes from that warning voice.
Bitter dark chocolate.

My Italy, your England.
        Long, white sleeves intervene:
table whisked clean.

Turning from quarrel.
        Fountain, pitcher, glass, lips, tongue:
the plash of water.

9

Dantic, Miltonic chords.
        An apple falling on a wooden floor.
Her eyes show decision.

An ice cube rises
        from the bottom of the glass,
Cracks....

Tannic epics and red wine.
        Waiter stands aside, listening.
My voice, hers.

10

Waiter: "Abandon all
        used dishes, you who've eaten here."
He treads Dante's steps.

"I've never understood
        The snake in ante-Purgatory.
How was your dessert?"

Tables nearly emptied.
      The waiter sits with us.
Dark eyes narrow, flash.

11

"Scholars *agonistoi*."
      He raises an index finger,
retrieves a dark bottle.

Achilles, Aeneas—
      scales in perfect balance.
The wine: Opus One!

She must have her Milton,
      I my Dante.
Orchids beside the roses.

12

Swirl of purple musk.
      Lush strains of Vivaldi die out.
The clink of glasses.

Where two giants meet,
      the beetle and the sparrow,
both scratch the dust.

As we linger, drink:
      the lace of thoughts and voices.
Lily petals on white cloth.

CHAUCER THE VINTNER

(poems of medievalism)

Wine Merchant's Son

And Chaucer's lips are lock'd
in piping London Middle English
with songs of wine and love and death,
politically tactful, and so tactical
in business, so savvy and practical,
his stories true-ish,
his shelves well stocked,
his characters breathe depth and breadth,
chests of treasures packed beyond measure.

Red and white and dry and sweet,
friend to nightingales and owls, too,
and hardly a nudged retreat through
three kings: sold his wines, shared his lines,
avoided jail and even fines
praising the good few
while filling each mews and street
with bowls of sharp satire:
enjoy his praise; avoid his ire.

Sir Sellivane and the Solitary Beast

The story and the knight you know,
tales from the time of Thomas Aquinas:
not quiet Pellinore and his Questing Beast,
nor Arthur and the Round Table's finest.

Not Isold' and Tristan, Elaine and Lancelot;
Richard-the-Lion nor Robert the Devil;
nor Galahad's faith, nor Gawain's failing,
nor King of Fools, nor Queen of Revels,

nor mightiest of mortals, nor meek-as-maid
Gawain, grandest of the Orkneys,
bold Gareth, his brother and better,
nor Norse Volsungs or bearish Bjorkings.

Known as Sir Selli to his friends and sisters,
hardiest of riders, hardly a Thopas,
none else goes so Errant, humble not envious,
the ladies all said, "Too well-mannered to grope us."

Sir Selli serenely endured sorrows,
more magnanimously accepted misery:
this sole knight sought the Solitary Beast,
he who like Perceval proved his woodcraft,

won victories in waste lands
where courtier would cower, deprived and cold.
Blue blood of ancient ages,
he never loved the life of court,

Full of f foppish folk, all fawning there.
Only he dared follow that deadliest foe,
hungriest of horrors, hoariest of monsters
that makes all human comfort morbid,

the one that swallows up the soul.
Girded for battle, and privileged in glory,
eager to eye his awful antagonist,
ascetic in tastes and artful in conflict,

Sir Sellivane rode through the slashing heat,
cutting cold and cruel storm,
donned the hair shirt and feasted on duty
through comfortless nights and famished noons

over windswept rocks, though winding woods,
in the tireless silence of the leafless trees.
Free of filched glances in flowery gardens:
no soft-skinned maids, no courtly manners

no soft beds nor singing hearth-fires
soothed his sufferings. Seldom on the path
he found chapel or hermitage, cottage or homestead,
and all he disdained, dedicated to his promise:

to avoid the mead-hall, the joust or merrymaking.
Beside a high-walled abbey the gatekeeper hailed him,
asked in hospitality if he would hear mass;
Sir Sellivane waved thanks and went his way.

He questioned a carter at a quiet burg
if anyone had word of woe wrought by the beast;
the poor fellow merely scratched his forehead:
he had never heard of such harrowing creatures.

Sharp cliffs over the battered shore,
high moors and the marshy bog
made his haunts, dripping moss
near the steep cataract, deep snows

on the mountain peaks. Poets' myths,
knightly jests, and peasant japes
fell into the past. The vow he pursued
the raw saint's quest centered his thoughts.

The trodden way, dung-card track,
the creaky inn, the odor of decay,
plaited hair and patterned sword,
all that shaped and unshaped, that shamed

or civilized, became to him as chain or bane.
The quest at once enslaves and frees,
frees of others, enslaves to self.
For years and days he dedicated his labors,

firm of spirit, passion all spent.
The beast, elusive, fled before him,
not dragon-hoard or haughty castle
set so one can surely find it, settled far

or near as end to his quest to terminate the ache
of seeking. Yet seek he did, Sir Sellivane;
he sought and sought that Solitary Beast
with little hope to find and no thought of home.

Temperate he proved, and chaste and true,
he searched the forest, strand, and sea
as best he might to test his mettle,
untiring, brave, yet the Solitary Beast

would ever flee, a day, an instant,
a week, a month, a year, a moment
away, ahead always of the weary questor.
Boldly still he searched, as he believed he should—

Committed to a course, one must never quail—
for what, he mused, he wanted most,
for what he felt he had to find,
for what in fact he always had,

the solitude that brought both solace
and suffering, certainty of deedless deeds
that blunt no swords and break no hearts,
so stoic ever, Sir Sellivane.

The Miraculous Marriage of Marakesh, Medieval Moorish Maiden

Part 1 of *Twelve Medieval Morish Maidens*

(Trans. from North-African Arabic by E. P. Unum, M.A, Ph.D., R. S., N.E.M.O.)[1]

Since the siege of Spain was squelched and scoured,
Valencia enveiled in oranges, Andaluz in artichokes,
A long age ere the arrival of Abe Lincoln, Vampire Hunter,
A maiden so modest and merry, and not at all mouthy
Sailed keenly from Morocco to Madrid, I know not how,
Borne thence on an ass of her own to Barcelona,
From there by barque to Arthur's Britain, Mighty Isle,
For the main sake of adventure, and maybe marriage.
Her hair as glossy as star-strewn Arabian nights,
Her feet small and soft, her figure fine, her eyes
As bright as dew in April that falls on the grass,
The whites at least. The pupils were dark as night,
As black as I know not what, but something quite black,
Perhaps as nun's habit, or as light when there's none.
Her teeth, her soul, her toenails truly as white
As pearls, as ice caps, as ice cream, as sea foam,
Or something much whiter than those, I'm not sure.
Her thoughts full of wisdom, her tongue quick with wit,
Her pure heart packed with percipience and pleasure

---

1   From British Library ms. Cotton Maximillian V8.

        And joy.
        For love of God she traveled,
        Some grateful guy to win.
        Her virtue ne'er unraveled,
        Free of guilt and sin.

Marakesh was her name, maiden Moor. Much to her Mother's
Distaste and her father's uproar she set out to determine
What day and what hour she should wed wise Manawyddan
Of the Isle of Britain, unaware he wasn't a Moor.
Boldly his broad face appeared in her magic mirror,
Great gift to have from Merlin or Gandalf, or in a pinch got
From any reputable antique market or Kasbah in north Africa
Or Asia Minor. Not leastwise muddled, but memorably clear
He appeared, to the highlights of his bushy blond beard.
Taught by sound sages to study the secrets,
She glimpsed his mug in the miracle glass, gathered her feelings
And thoughts to interpret its intricate images. She knew
Right away that the face that emerged so easy to see
Belonged to her husband-to-be, or someone like him.
She knew as if she'd met him the bold blue eyes,
The kind expression, the nifty crown on the brink of his brow,
The wisdom, much like her own, that shone in his smile
        So bright.
        And so she set off sailing
        With a keen well-mannered crew.
        As a medieval Moorish princess,
        What else could she choose to do?

This Medieval Moorish maiden, maturing as she went,
Sailed boldly where no such one had sailed before,
As I said above, but now with more illuminating details:
She Paused in Spain for shopping, for savory outfits
To fill out her trousseau and treat her lovely tresses
And smooth skin with all the latest luxuries,
Exfoliants, hydrations, lathers, creams, and balms,
Mostly for protection against weather (a girl must know her products),
But also to treat true crew and servants to lunch and tea,
Elevensies, and B & B's, for bounteous and generous she was

(I hate to end a line of poetry with *was*).
And next, since they were traveling anyway, they strayed
To Venice, Florence, to meet foreign sibyls,
Hear soothsayers say sooth, or something encouraging,
The Riviera, Paris with its shops and pretty dainties,[2]
Alps for skiing, Bologna for spaghetti sauce
(I may have erred and got some stops misordered),
To Belgium for beautiful cloth, and baths for everyone.
Berlin chefs offered sauerbraten: she politely declined.
In Worms one of her crew got worms; a healer cured him.
But almost all the stops were fun and educational, for she
> Was wise.
> Marakesh made much of travels,
> Saw all the sights she could.
> With such indulgent parents,
> Any traveler would!

So then laden with knowledge, treats, and treasures,
This Manawyddan mindful Marakesh sought[3]
Through all provinces, paltry or pretty, of the West Isles
Till her swift ship settled on Cymric shores, Wales to some,
Though she'd seen real whales on the way. Under the welkin
In the land of the dragon and Pendragon persisted our princess.
She searched at Llangammarch, Llanuwchllyn, and Llanerchymedd,
Rested at Rhyddhywel, Renmaermawr, and Rhosllanerchrugog,
Ate lunch at Aberystwyth, mounted Mynydd Eppynt,
Climbed Carnedd Llewelyn, sent a post card from
> Pontrhydfendigaid—

It had a really big stamp—that she bought at Hay-on-Wye,
In a nifty bookshop, which made her think of her parents. I don't
> know why.

One day she came at last to Dyfed, where she met Manawyddan,
Great man, long sought for and much admired, worthy mentor and
> kind,

---

2   The translator takes no responsibility for insipid phrases.
3   The translator has in several instances kept the syntax or lexical tone of the original, however odd to the English reader, to maintain the flavor of the poem. In this case obviously Marakesh sought Manawyddan.

But found he'd got old, was married with children, and wasn't a
    Muslim,
Which of course made the marriage impossible. But they did
Invite her to a nice dinner of turnips and tatties, salads and pasties,
And cheese and rabbit, which I'm told tastes like cheese and chicken.
Then must Marakesh re-think her plan and go home or find a new
    man
                To marry.
                Not so easy to deter
                A medieval Moorish princess.
                She sought a mosque to pray
                And burnt some expensive incense.

On her way from mosque, the one at Tintern, just above Wye,
Hard by the great abbey of Wordsworth's nice poem, not a large one,
That mosque, but sufficient for prayer, she met a bard, Blwchfardd by
    name,
Son on Aneirin, the son of Taliesin, better bards than the great
    Merlin,
This tulk, who the trammes of treason there wrought, that made him
    barmy,
This Blwch had a magic mirror better than her own—they're
    untrustworthy, you know.
Blwchfardd had foreseen her coming, and he knew her quest:
He advised her to ride for Northumberland where, as all know,
There's a much bigger mosque in the lands of young King Ælla.
This Ælla descended from that Alla known to all readers of ancient
Chaucer from his Man of Law's Tale. Alla converted for Constance,
His wife, to Christianity and traveled to Rome to recover
The woman he found so dear, once his mother had chucked her out.
Our Ælla, also a nice guy, had as ancestor the bold brother
Of Alla: he abided in Northumbria, held true to Islam,
Built a great Mosque, later begat legions of goodly Muslims
There in Northern lands. This maiden lad, a king already,
Looked much like Manawyddan, but younger, brown of beard,
Bold of face, with sky blue eyes and teeth as white as—
We've been through this; you know what white looks like—
And black of hair, black as the raven, as Welsh coal,
As a squash that's sat out in the sun for a long time, a very long time.

And except for all that he appeared just like Manawyddan, almost,
              As I've said.
              You've never seen man so handsome
              As this sterling Muslim lad.
              A kinder, gentler monarch
              Old Britain had never had.

Over fells and moors and marshes meek Marakesh made way,
Riding on a new ass she'd purchased on Chester's Market day,
In saner days, when good asses could be bought without surgery.
On her way she met pilgrims plodding off somewhere,
And for a time she joined their jog to hear stories, news, and jokes.
One famous tale she liked of a rooster and a fiendish fox:
The mammal tricks the bird to bow his head and belt out
Some show-tune, and the fine fellow seizes Chaunticleer
And dashes down the lane. Dead-sure of his catch,
He turns to taunt the chasers. Less truant now in action,
The bird escapes his open mouth. "Awa," says the cock,
"I shallna go wi' thee again"—I think he was a Scot.
At that merry tale maid Marakesh laughed (or loughed),
But not out loud, and covered her lips, to keep propriety.
She also heard a joke about a priest, minister, and Rabbi,
But couldn't recall it after, though sure she'd thought it funny.
Soon the pilgrims went their way, not wending for Northumbria,
So Marakesh endured alone again except for guards and sailors,
Her fortune-teller, manicurist, her bowling partner, and hair-dresser,
              As one needs.
              The well-accoutered princess
              Must prepare for any need
              If she's to find a husband
              Worth marrying indeed.

Not in Nottingham, hardly in Huddersfield, less yet in Leeds
She found her love. Bad luck in Bradford, hard times in Harrogate
She found, but napped at Knaresborough, watched the Bed Race,
Famous festival, through the city streets and across the water,
Backtracked to York for pudding, put in to Scarborough, had parsley
At the fair and thyme—they'd used up all the sage—and trotted
Up the coast at last, carefully to camp along Northumbrian Tyne.

Near Newcastle, with its famous brew, did not imbibe, good girl,
But ached for Ælla, composed a sonnet, or sestina it may have been,
That, sadly, did not survive. As luck would go, at lunch one day
She heard the king had housed at Hexham, and off she hurried
With all her train in tow, with one last tourist stop
To see Hadrian's Wall—who wouldn't—but missed the Housesteads
        latrine,
Built with room for two dozen Roman bums at once.
And when at last she saw the Hexham gates, they stood thrown wide:
For Ælla awaited her, able king and seer—he had a magic mirror, too.
He had seen his bride-to-be, had sent brave scouts around
To find her, but they had somehow missed. Destiny goes undenied,
If one believes such silly things. When Marakesh spied him
And he viewed her, they knew at once the verity of vision,
Found each other fully foxy, in a chaste and prudent way.
Even Ælla's sainted (in a Muslim way) mother thought Marakesh
        A Darling.
        They named their wedding day.
        And plighted troth together;
        You could have knocked each over
        With the touch of a feather.

So the merry couple married in the marvelous mosque.
They honeymooned a month in Rome and Rimini. Ravenna
They caught, cadged a week with royalty in Constantinople.
Then on they made for Morocco, to meet the bride's parents,
Who sighed with relief and joy to see their sunny daughter
Wed to such a fine Islamic lad, the kind and lordly Ælla,
Both dressed in white, whiter than white—I've seen nothing so white.
Their people east to west, and north to south,
All except a few inveterate tourists, whom no one pleased,
Celebrated for another month, paused but for holy days.
Refreshed, solaced, they turned at last again for Britain,
Green and pleasant land, where in they settled
As the kindest, gentlest, most eager to praise
Of all rulers of their time, and of most other times, too.
They had nice kids, pretty smart, who wrote the final verses
To their story in years to come, but never learned alliteration.
And so their story ends, since happiness makes poems

That remain best simple and short: big problems make best tales.
                        That's it.
                        May all such Moorish maidens
                        Find princes good and fair,
                        And all such faltering poets
                        Be remembered in your prayers.

Deor

(translated from Old English)

Weland himself knew the worm's persecution,
hardy man, in hardship experienced;
he had for companions sorrow and longing,
wintercold wretchedness, often-felt woe,
since Niðhad fetched him in fetters,
supple sinew-bonds on the better man.
                That passed; so may this.

Nor was Beadohild for her brother's death
in heart so sore as she was for own suffering,
once she had clearly conceived
that she was pregnant. Never could she
calmly consider how that must come out.
                That passed; so may this.

We learn that Mæðhild's moans
rose grievously, Geat's lady,
how sorrow-love stripped them of all sleep.
                That passed; so may this.

Theodorich spent thirty winters
in the Mærings' fastness—that was known to many.
                That passed; so may this.

We have all learned of Eormanric's
wolfish thought, widely ruled folk
of the Gothic kingdoms: that was a grim king!
Many a man sat moored in sorrows,
Expecting woe, constantly wishing
that kingdom were overcome.
        That passed; so may this.

The sorry one sits deprived of joys,
made gloomy in spirit; it seems to himself
his griefs grow endless in number.
So may it seem that throughout this world
the Wise Lord wends always,
to many men shows honor,
certain fame, to others great woes.

So I wish to say for myself
that I for a while was the Heodening's scop,
dear to my lord. *Deor* was my name.
I had many years a good office,
a gracious lord, but now Heorrenda,
song-crafty man, has got the place
the protector of earls once gave to me.
        That passed; so may this.

Wulf and Eadwacer

(translated from Old English)

To my folk it is as if one offers them a sacrifice.
They will kill him if he comes with a host.
    It is different for us.
Wulf is on one island, I on another.
Fast is that island, surrounded by fens.
They are slaughter-mad, the men on that island.
They will kill him if he comes with a host.
    It is different for us.
Of my Wulf's wanderings I thought hopefully
when it was rainy weather, and I sat weeping.
Then the battle-bold one belayed me with arms.
There was joy in that; there was loathing, too.
Wulf, my Wulf! Your hopes,
so few visits, made me sick,
mourning in mind, not the least hungry.
Do you hear, Eadwacer? Our wretched whelp
Wulf bears off to the woods.
One easily parts what never was joined,
our song together.

Almsgiving
(translated from Old English)

Well be the man, just-minded one,
who has inside him a spacious heart:
that gets from the world greatest honor
and from the Lord the best of Fame.
Even as with water he would extinguish
welling flame, that it might no further
harm his borough, burning brightly,
so with alms me he cast away all
the scars of sin, heal his soul.

Metrical Preface to Gregory's Pastoral Care

(translated from Old English)

This errand-message   Augustine the missionary
brought from the south   over the salt sea
to island-dwellers,   just as it was dictated
beforehand   to the Lord's leader,
the Pope of Rome.   Many righteous speeches
bright-minded Gregory   pored over,
through his wise heart, a hoard of learned thoughts.
Thus he of all men   turned the most folk
to the Sky's Guardian,   that best of Romans,
richest in spirit,   most renowned for glories.
Kling Alfred   afterward translated
each word of me   into English,
sent north and south   and commanded his scribes
that they make more of me,   that they might send
them to his bishops,   since some might need it,
those who least knew Latin.

Middle Voice

for Diane Legomsky

Middle voice
doesn't mean
no one takes action.
Action happens anyway,
"Action!" lush or lean,
holds sway.

Friendship often happens
in middle, not passive voice.
You give, I give;
friendship takes over, varies
plots its course, its tributaries,
bends, smooths how we live.

"Fortune can't take away
what you give your friends,
what they give you":
Martialis' voice gives us voice.
Voice, active or middle, dear friend:
free will: a choice.

from ON SHAKESPEARE, IN SONNETS

Will of Stratford

England's pyramid, and her Colossus,
greatest Garden, verbal empire, Rock,
Alexandrian library, heart, Knossos,
best son, voice, preferred stock…
We love lists, and any list of "greatest"
names him first, Warwickshire lad,
despite pretenders, or the late or latest
fad's contenders, or any feckless cad's
assertion his ancestor wrote Will's plays.
Emerging talent always mystifies,
whether it comport in wisdom, art, or lays,
like a new rose brilliant to our eyes.
He lit our envy, wit, and deep desires.
A magister. A writer's Muse of Fire.

The End of Lear

A thousand years of learning wouldn't help:
a feather or a glass would tell as much
an any ECG. The primordial yelp
tells the whole story. He can't touch
what we already know: no phoenix lives
in that limp body. And not the general
mortality has got her, the death that gives
us commonality, but pride, that venerable
foe, first enemy, straight from her parent.
The old Zen koan: grandfather, father,
son die, in proper order: coherent
patterns make pain bearable. Bother,
worry, edit as you will: earth galls
with Lear's cry. The final curtain falls.

The Financier of Venice

Her betrayal hurt the most: her turning,
and for a boy who didn't even love her.
He chewed on the money to forget the burning,
feckless, as an eyeless hawk would hover,
in jaw-drop agony at the rose withered.
Jessica, like Portia and Nerissa,
had no idea of love. Like them she dithered
away wealth, honor, self. Miss a
bleating, selfish lover? Who ever does?
The Merchant, plaintiff, monster, casts a glance—
where? Gold, silver, lead, he makes a buzz
louder than a rich bride whose chance
for freedom fades. Venice turns at last
itself a devil, and we watch all aghast.

After Romeo and Juliet

If Romeo had won his Rosaline

and Juliet met Paris at the masque;
had Lear to daughters' motives been less blind,
Hippolytus taken Phaedra less to task;
were Tamburlaine at ease in Scythian wood,
had Faustus found contentment in his books
and Webster's Duchess rest in widowhood
and Hamlet peace in sweet Ophelia's looks:
would we be one day different, you and I,
one clasp closer, one kiss kinder now,
one tear less lost for all the world's flood?
Would centuries of introspection cry
less loudly, were we more faithful to a vow,
less eager, hungry, at the smell of blood?

Coda

When to the taints of fortune and despair
I once again bequeath my teeming fears,
allow my heart and every passing care
to tendril through the spent, now lifeless years,
then comes so silkily the thought that words
can't matter, that deep down they change
nothing, said or read. Such fancy girds
the nerves, but blunts imagination's range.
But Will, on stage or in the mind, persists,
like the choric thrush repeats his song,
his eyes dispassionately fixed, insists
on nothing, hinting everything, so long
as we can breathe and eyes can see.
The votive candle burns perpetually.

from SONGS OF THE CITY (1989)

Uptown Ballad

Restaurant uptown, way up north:
lights flicker low.
fillet mignon hisses with attitude,
waitresses in short skirts smile familiarly.

In an Irish pub:
the twang of the taut-strung bow
bends Republican songs to a knife's edge.
A Corvette and a Harley wait outside.

Café carved in an old railroad terminal:
eight-point buck,
booth built like a caboose,
cigar-store Indian hidden in the back,
blush-cheeked porcelain dancing girl
by the door with her red-lipped smile.

I listen carefully:
"Live!" she says. "Live!"

Nocture

Smoky evening creeps from its concrete tomb:
ebony river's steady cymbals glisten, pity
presbyopic night, shoot deep
glances at blinking skies. A painted face
makes promises it cannot keep
as soft jazz breathes billows,
begs grace from sepulchral streets.
Alley-bent echoes rumble, die.

Steps tap, quiet as mausoleum visitors,
quicken through doors, and pass.
Faint stars ember coal-scuttle heights,
trumpet-mute thin light into the fog.
Sagging clouds condemn, quick-glanced,
guilty inquisitors from grimy hotels
off shadow-laden corners. The cold river's sigh
draws in. Stark mill stacks pierce a falling sky.

Fall of the City

Jab-scarred city rises like a boxer from the canvas.
Sueted, vengeful, swollen-faced demi-god
of bygones breathes staccato, breast heaving.
Open-mouthed streets pant and sweat,
swill reek, moil in banks of moonlight.
Concrete contenders grow muscular and quick
in damp, cruel air; heat spins and dodges
into cramp corners of blood-red brick.

Taxi horns hook, weave and wrench,
cars uncrouch, cross and cut in forays;
careening traffic, merciless in battle roil,
flayed in hot echoes of nightly throes,
fire, battle, buckle, whistle sapped jazz.
Gusts writhe round churchtop steeples,
grunt, swear, plead for power, seep
into sewers swelled with river-wrought woes.

City seethes under fistic wind's blows,
breezes circle, clinch, whip body-
punches, gouge like stray thumbs through
through tenements, closed galleries, and alleys.
Steps, steady on split pavement, sound the count.
    Moonlight pushes strangers, horns cheer
    offkey. Ghostly hands flail,
        plead, wild in flat-cast lamplight.

Rise of the City

Out from under the hill,
from roughed cobble and grey asphalt,
out of the soul-deep darkness,
the tap-root temple of thin tree-lawns,
out of once hallowed hollows,
out of the rank, sewered corners,
the feckless ways
the grave,
the endlessly turning quietless streets,
I waken.

Take counsel, empty bottles and silenced fountains,
hear the whisper pasted on bronzed dawn.
Take note, pawned instruments, stopped watches:
out of its fifty-year midnight
The City rises.
I rise.

Past the staunch steel of rusted bridges
once flashing in the sun, puissant with traffic,
the living City cries like a birth,
a heave from the hips of its own hills,
from the swell of the river
tumbling out from umbilical quadrangles,
fertive and fertile and flailing,
washing in its own, old, pent-up tears.

Reborn, the City and I,
freeing ourselves from ourselves, our dying demons,
the broken lenses of time and name,
finding each our old companion, old confessor,
brothers and mutual tyrants in fear and pain,
now each a phoenix from the past's proleptic ashes.

Song of the City

When the blood rush of new hopes calms,
and day's gloss fades like youth,
the City, faithful as true lover,
ready as a roving eye,
moody as a pouting lip,
pants like a third-set dancer
or a fourth-lap miler
or a spent prophet.

A jazz band bends all streets
into an old honky-tonk
where time slows to a love-whisper.
Drums low-rumble, sax brags, bass swags
in the tongue of the streets and the street people;
song-merchant, soft and persistent
as a loving-heart's beat,
waves, twirls, bows, bends melodies into braids,
and piano soli dive and splash, swim and mingle.

Night wind, first gentle as a sleeping breath,
tender as skilled hands touching a flute,
builds now, tumbles a freed leaf
like a gymnast, melts the ice of anger,
pops enmity like a Champagne cork.
       How good to feel the rain,
       the thrilling ease of cold beer,
       the bite and brogue of hot black coffee,
       to hear the winged jazz ring though the crippled, living
streets.

from AMONG DUSTY SHELVES (1994)

Introit

Begin. *Te Deum*
Ease. *hymnus*
Clear. *qui tolis peccata*
Hear. *in aeternam*

grant bridges and byways
grant domed words for poems,
ripe words, red words,
words that jut, that tremble, that bay
grant the space between words, between lines,
the space between poems
to navigate the lag,
the space where I can't say, don't see,
grant life and heart for poems,
ego to make poems,
freedom from the me that makes poems
grant poems that sprout and climb,
that crash and rumble and burst,
visceral poems, contemplative poems,
poems that sing, that shout, that
break
poems that stretch, dash, scale, pare
poems of rivers and trains,
of people, people, and people
poems out of dark corners,

poems alight with wings,
with thorns, with wounds,
poems that bleed, that heal, that love

amen, amen

resurgit.

Hamlet Erect

or, What Hamlet Said to Ophelia before He Left

O those O those
primordial perpetual archetypal omphalical curves
how they
even now
like swinging ships
inspire such fire
O linger, linger
until all slinging quips retire

Do let me touch
just there again

too soon to quench
just yet
dear noonday desire

Rest with me
let's try again:
easy, now, and
slow

Overheard: Woman's to the Lover She Left

By a feeble fire, with an unread book,
it is cold, and my thoughts are gusts

I try to trust the fading words,
though eyes' hours fly, and ears forget.

Bones know only chill winds for true,
fingers numb to sinewy embers.

On clamp-jawed nights thoughts like gusts
blow, linger, fall.

Snow chips away at window-frost;
sparks quail from the hearth-breeze.

Blind battering cracks at the shutters;
memories curse, cry, and die.

I trust no books, nor all such bitter things:
words waver by failing candlelight.

Frost builds new half-circles,
quarter-moons on the pane.

Ice cuts the wretched sills,
and the last hearth-flames genuflect.

Cold chains fallow night,
and dawn's empty womb shudders.

Night's cords draw tight:
it is cold, and my thoughts are gusts

Postlude

Why did Dante write a Beatrice,
Petrarch a Laura that he never kissed?
I'd rather kiss, then write,
then kiss again—
maybe keep silent—
leave a little of the kiss
in the writing,
keep a little bliss
for moments like this.

May you always have poems.
May I always have poems.
May you always have kisses.
May I always have kisses.

And when the weary lip
settles into sleep,
may the stopped tongue
dance among the stars.
and remaining eyes
remember you, remember me,
our voices wander where they must,
and our few lines together flower in the dust.

from LIGHT ON STONE (2004)

NYC, Fall 2001

Weeds beneath a redwood would feel this way:
        hardy, overwhelmed, misplaced, if they
        could feel, like tourists too poor to stay
        long, gazing, self-conscious, into the fray.
        What subway joins, let no one pull asunder.

Above, a city, emasculated, throbbing, sutures
        itself bravely not so much to health
        as, knowing its marrow our future,
        to mass produce again culture and wealth,
        breeding at times light, horror, wonder.

Monuments

Edinburgh castle, stolid
  as an ivory-faced judge,
   bolts hill to the clouds grey as the North Sea.
West, the Giant's Causeway, solid
  as tides permit, refuses to budge;
   sludge may stain burn and brae,
  but green atones.

Roman Wall, prosthetic
  upon sinuous hogbacks,
   watches north, south, as Hadrian asked,
except where men in their aesthetic
  tore it from sweat-mortared stacks
  to make sheep wall or churches, tasked
  for fresh stone.

Salisbury Plain: barrows
  like gooseflesh mottle
   the distance around stark Stonehenge,
dolmans tumbled by those who harrow
  holy places and try to bottle
  what the Cathedral in revenge
  does with light.

In Canterbury a red *X*
  marks the martyr's spot;
   other martyrs' faces grace the apse.
Off Dover from the decks
  of ships soldiers sought
  comfort from Cliffs that without lapse
  shine white:

The comfort of light sparking off familiar stone.

Gosforth Cross

Three miles off the Irish Sea
two cultures met and crossed
in a single monument, still free-
standing in a Cumbrian churchyard.
Somehow surviving unmarred
Henry's depredations, it's lost
nothing of its native power, though
the context faded centuries ago:
fourteen feet of loam-dark
stone bearing Oðin/Christ
and Valkyrie/Mary, for when the spark
of old ways no longer sufficed.

Master sculptor, working alone,
must, pulling back from his hot chisel,
have felt something wholly remarkable:
that light had crept into his stone.

What the Thunder Said

"…and I heard a voice from heaven saying, 'seal up the things which the seven peals of thunder have spoken, and do not write them.'"
--Revelation 10:4

After a storm, the sky's scorpion tale,
plunged, retracts, and quivering earth sighs.
Thunder, having spoken its piece, merely mutters
in the distance, and mist rises from the gutters
like smoke from a censer. A half-hour's silence,
and a hazy sun draws earthworms to the surface.
A row of olive trees glows in the thick air,
clouds recede, and the ancient, spectral arch
lights river and sky in passing peace.

"Give alms, show compassion, know self-control":
the message to the Waste Land from world war,
from a prophet such as we have in a tired age.
Love Canal, Chernobyl, Valdez, the fiery rage
of Saudi oil wells scorching the clouds:
bodies, burnt or burning, rain as ashes ever
since. Rwanda, Kosovo, Timor: peace passes
our understanding. A mother sends her children
back to play in the wet grass, or on the beach,
after the rain, or after ashes, till more fall,
to build castles of roots, sand, or stone.

Millions, billions of us, rainforests or not,
long-timers or not, muse in the thinning air,
watch while the rain spends itself, then dance
in the puddles—or, yes, ashes. History or
not, art or not, poetry or not, we forget our
umbrellas. The Old, longing for the light,
catch cold; the Young, impatient for a slight
chance, dance amid the stones. The Old will
prophesy, and—we persist, you know—the Young will
dream dreams: dreams of light and stone.

from A SECOND CITY STREET PROPHET SINGS THE BLUES

Night Scene

Where they sing the blues,
you and I sang the blues, sing the blues—
where all roads meet and all roads end,
where morning's a dream and noon's a bad trip
and night's a mother or a father or a lover
and everything that's not a shadow
gets ground under foot.

Banshee els skim peace from the night,
pierce 2 a.m. with living sparks
when they roar like trumpets into dying dreams.
The room sings with the weight of trains,
and the cracked mirror trembles.

Shiftless wind off the lake
slaps waves till they tumble
smooth and blue-black as midnight,
pitch rumbly notes
rich as the smell of your hair.
I tinker with my old words, your old words
and settle under the moon-strafed skyline
distant as trampling dawn.

Church Steeple

The honed point of the dome-top steeple
points fixedly at the sky,
stands proud and doughty;
sun streaks the steeple gold
like a stone-eyed priest's crozier
or Crusader's blade.

People point to the dome-top steeple
from lot and lawn
as grand bells wrangle
in the sand-blasted belfry.
An old blind man sits on the corner
selling pencils.

Street Scene

On certain November nights
wind clangs headless off the lake;
quick-as-a-heartbeat-cold waves
resound through the downtown,
echo in iron-still backstreets,
and frontrunning shop windows
wrack and ping in the sleet.

> The serrated old pencil man
> shuffles against stone-wind,
> his dull eyes frozen open;
> lake howls, sky heaves,
> and the wrinkled night pants for breath.

Commuter Train at Evening

Here again, here again: first by eye,
we tour the bridges.
Selves, highways, trains—all bridges.

Low over water City smoke hangs,
phantom in the wind.
Desiring eye pales
through grimy windows.
Foundry stack spits fire
at a gasping sky.

Downtown trains sweep
splayed and ragged
through concrete blinders,
swallow rails,   scorch slagged tracks
with wheel-spark incendiaries'
urban bellows' emphysemic air
drains and pools, roars and sputters.

Englobed in soot, trudging Dreams
of shuffling boots and thick coats
dangle onto station platforms
when cars lurch and doors thrust to—
and only naked patience
shuts the screeching wind.

Top to Bottom

City night lights
cut street-shores fjord-like
into Tartarean bridges.

Breath-
      less
            surf
waves of innocence
      through serpentine neon.

Windows strobe
at the fluttering rush,
edged winds break
from the north,

and a pale worm nibbles
at a corner tenement.

Pilgrimage

Juan de la Cruz sits quietly
sprawled under a bo tree,
rolls down his tube socks,
face upturned to a chattering muezzin.

Down the long road
he sees, knows the hunched shoulders,
flings an arrow with all his might—
then turns his discalced heart away.

From his grassy shrine, he snickers as I go.
Oh, I've been watching, all right.

And for what he found
I keep searching the place
where logic fails, where words fail,
somewhere down night's empty alleys,
somewhere down memory's battered streets.

Raising the Dead

Far from Chicago Blues as you can still smell rusty morning,
Far from Detroit as you can roll mo' Motown R&B;
from Cleveland as you can still hear sere flames
    licking the Cuyahoga,
from Pittsburgh where black rivers meet, where millsmillsmills
    girded the sky with soot,
from Phily's South St. and Boston's Lenny's on the Turnpike,
from Harlem's once Cotton Club and still Apollo
    big as a whisper in someone else's ear,
from N' Orleans where sax cooks jam-balaya,
from Memphis' Beale Street voices handy on the keys,
from Frisco City Lights where beats scratch windfall notes
    from Gate to Rock to wharf,
from Atlanta's brave, scarlet streets and St. Louis screaming
    to the west:

    You can hear the blues pour like black, black coffee,
    singe the fog thick as gumbo
    and raise the dead:
                      Come back sweet Charlotte
                      Little Sheba
                      Amazing Grace
    to dig up Big Daddy buried in blues.

from THE STREETS OF HARMON FALLS

Small Town

(for Edgar Lee Masters and E. A. Robinson)

The river smells of sunk-eyed catfish,
and sludge bobs belly-up. The town broods
beneath the cemetery on the hill. The wish
of all the dozing willows, all the dudes
in suped-up cars: to crush those stones, uproot
them, rock, forget the iron-orange streams
that kill all they touch, deny the football star hanged himself. Dreams,
like union jobs in steel and coal, have died.
Weak ghosts of profligate congressmen huddle
in copses with shades of factory managers who lied
to laborers about working conditions. The muddle,
heave, and percussive rush of urban grief
they missed, where most folk live on Relief.

Walnut Grove

Here is a copse of quiet and of bones.
The aged stones are cracked and weathered smooth.
The willow branches form an arch: the gate
opens into the shadows where the moans
of autumn breezes through damp leaves would soothe
the bent and wind-worn walnut trees—too late,
the summer rose has burned to brown and rust.
They tell me this was once a battle site,
the dead youths scattered here and there.
The mosses on the ancient trees grow green,
and mushrooms sprout; can you imagine quite
what timely fruits these planted bones shall bear?
The tombstone faces are eroded clean.
The names, like cares, and joys, have blown to dust.

Stone Quarry

A stark, Druidic place, off-white and dun,
of eerie silhouettes. A shapeless sun
blights sterile slag, a site wise creatures shun,
a quarter mile from the woods and run.
Huge stones, sharp, tossed and heaped, disordered mass,
between two stones, a single blade of grass,
no more… The lake sits still as leaded glass,
deep blue: opaque as oxidizing brass.
A near-perverse, distorted beauty lies
upon the jagged crater and its beard
of dry and twisted roots. An open mouth,
its stony teeth reverberate the cries
of an indifferent crow, now disappeared,
come, curious, from meadows to the south.

The Hillside Tavern

Come to where the Hillside Tavern stood,
passed the way of every drop of time.
Days linger here, the streamlets wash and cover
rocks and clayey banks; eroding floods
will seldom trouble buried sand- or lime-
stone. Currents dwindle, storms pass, breezes hover
over hill and tumbling tavern's hall.
Upon the hillside, near its base, above
untroubled streams, the Hillside Tavern served
the local steelmen and miners, those
who worked their shifts, and, taxes paid, tried
to save enough for houses, cars. Time swerved
around them, evenings at the Hillside. Close
the rusty-hinged door: night's shadows fall.

St. John of Lost Son's Lane

Past a decrepit corner, down the hill
from the vaulted arches of the Catholic church,
on Lost Son's Lane by Unknown Soldier's Park,
he wanders, night or day and sun or chill:
an old, old man, he's called "St. John." Grey birch
trees line the park he saunters by; his dark
and aimless eyes weave hours from time's distaff.
Past the Union Hall and Fatty's Bar he stalks,
the baseball fields, the Armory, and back.
And when the shadow of the high church falls,
he lifts his head and mumbles as he talks
like an old priest praying, pants legs slack,
hands clasped before him, till the churchbell calls.
And the children skip after him and laugh.

May in Harmon Falls

May is the most beautiful month in Harmon
Falls: when grass glows green from gentle rain,
and birdsong flutters like a pipe organ's
breathy notes, and the air smells fresh again.
In fragrant May, the flowers fill with dew
like cups each early morning: evening brings
a red-brushed cloud-fringed sky as alive and new
as children's wishes, as swallows when they sing.
And budded trees emblazon afternoons
with leaf and flower; wild blooms fire
the meadows rolling in the hills, and the runes
of horned breezes pipe, lusty with desire.
And as the flood of May-wash ranges free,
old hopes and memories bloom, then die in me.

At a Bend in the River

The river shelters by a sycamore-
lined bank and forms a gentle bay at River's
bend. A steady slosh of wavelets calls
the listener. How the willows bow before
fall winds, and then a thousand linked rings shiver
from their droplets, when the soft rains fall,
that pock and pit, and mingle imperceptibly.
And when the drizzles stop, how smooth the flow,
how satiny the surface once again.
And when the moon hangs in the sky, predictably,
the raccoons waddle to the bank. The glow
at midnight hardly daunts the bullfrogs' plain-
song, or the crickets' chirrup, or the walk
of lovers quiet in their careless talk.

The Falls

Unlike many American small towns
with the name "Falls," dear Harmon Falls
has one, truly. Cleft clatter redounds
in the dells from high up the rocky walls
that sharpen as they peak, but tumble steep,
blasted back to dig room for the new
highway. In August the rumbles sleep;
quick flow dries to a trickle, nor any dew
feeds morning gold or evening silver to the dry
grasses or clinging trees. But in late autumn
or spring, when the rains teem, the parched eye
greets green Heaven would envy, and the bottom
rock below beats drums like a Highland corps
marching, as the wild waters' echoes roar.

Churches and Bars

Two dozen bars, two dozen
Churches, all within a mile or less:
small-town geography. Close cousin
to the church, a bar: greet, bow heads, confess,
pursue forgiveness, ask for hope from wine
and bread, or beer and burgers. Try not to think
of Monday. Sunday comes again, benign,
and Saturday with music, games, and drink.
Greek Orthodox, and Catholic, Pentecostal,
Presbyterian, Methodist, all preach the Gospel.
Prince's, Fatty Joe's, the Tiger Pub,
Drift Inn, and Lion's Den for booze and grub.
A song, a sermon, prayers in antiphon;
a Scotch or two, a laugh, and then we're gone.

Garden Memorial

No tombstones dot the quiet, emerald hill;
brass plates denote the clients sheltered there;
a modern chapel marks the hill's descent.
A large flag ripples overhead until
late evening, flashing stars, bold stripes. A spare
wind unfurls staid maples: a soft lament
accompanies their sigh, Light birch limbs wave.
Sleek Grecian statues strike an attitude
of still-life, tasteful art, and dignity;
new mounds are small and few, for by the chapel
stands a shrine for funeral urns. A mood
of kind gentility resolves the parti-
colored flowers to somber peace. Red-dappled
poppies decorate my father's grave.

Peach Tree

The backyard peach tree bore no fruit this year.
The leaves dress less in green and more in brown.
The trunk stiffens, dry of sap; the long limbs tear,
and branches bend: long winters bear them down.
The wrens still linger, resting here in spring;
the days still plod with regularity.
The evergreens grow still; the crickets sing.
Summer wanes, and falls sings threnody.
My favorite peach tree bore no fruit this year.
A late swallow drops from a gust and cries.
The sounds of youth fall hollow on my ear.
The wrinkles deepen at my brow and eyes.
On the nearby hill the tombstones crumble, too.
The willows, like old sextons, wait their cue.

Hometown, Late

Change chews at things, surface and core,
even to their nature, eventually wearing
laws as well as leaves thin and sore.
While roots finger their way, tearing
loam ponderously, all the way to water,
and limbs trope to landscape, jaws, and wind,
deep down nature worms its slaughter
finer than cells, to branch, creep, rescind.
Knowing so makes more present field and block,
streetlight and store, wood and angling stream,
in this place far from events that mow and rock
the world; they stay the whole, like joist or beam.
So long enduring, fixed, yet not immune:
the town I knew has disappeared too soon.

from
THROUGH A GLASS DARKLY

Beach Arrivals

Sand grass floods the dunes, shivers with seabreeze;
first tern shoots oblique ease
as wind whisks a hang glider sure
off a cliff—we depart the before.

Lip of sun blows stars off the wine-white water,
and gulls spin for food in the after;
crossed crests dance in the key of C
as clear wash brings numinous me to me.

Butterfly

Like a butterfly my thoughts sip
at the red lip of the open-mouthed rose;
like a butterfly at the tulip's tip
they whirl till the spread wings close.

Like a butterfly my thoughts drift
to the water lily and the honeysuckle
and the hilly meadows, where breezes lift
clouds from the misty run, and small falls trickle

sweet water to the greening valley.
Like a butterfly my thoughts meander
far from the tumble-down alleys
and dust-laden streets they were wont to wander.

Woods at Dusk

Sun roosts on pedestal hill,
douses day brazen.
Mother night encumbers
till he falls chill;
dark day draws diapason
while whippoorwill chants numbers.

Eyes squirrel; hearts hasten.
Moonlight thrill
spills red song
over ivories, chasten-
blushed cheek. Chatter runs still
till hills spread wide and long.

Grandmother

She lifts fallen petals
in memoriam her cheeks' borrowed bloom.
Knotty fingers smooth the ground below
    Kyrie eleison

A hallowed garden of roses,
peonies, and azaleas, distant lilac:
petals drip like blood
    Kyrie eleison

In the kitchen alone
she removes gauzy gloves,
sips a glass of white wine,
stirs it with a rose stem
    Kyrie eleison
    Christe eleision

POSTSCRIPT

A Little Night Music

A little beeboppin' and doowoppin':
shoobop doo bop
nananananananananananana

Dit dit dit da
pa pa pa pa
dit dit dit da
pa pa pa pa
dit dit dit DA!

When you come near, can you hear?
shortshortshort long, long, long shortshortshort

the King, the Queen,
the LOUD, the lean

calm them muddy waters
oh black water
one more Jeremiad
sweet LR swingin' a Louisiana moon

solid rockin' gold…

LIGHTS OUT! I'M NOT TELLING YOU AGAIN!

Through the grapevine
I can hear clearly now
From 59th St. bridge
the sound of untroubled water

Let us rest
in the snore of the Dragon.

OTHER ANAPHORA LITERARY PRESS TITLES

White Shoes
By: Edward S. Louis

Notes for Further Research
By: Molly Kirschner

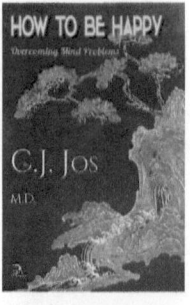

The Encyclopedic Philosophy of Michel Serres
By: Keith Moser

The Visit
By: Michael G. Casey

How to Be Happy
By: C. J. Jos

A Dying Breed
By: Scott Duff

Love in the Cretaceous
By: Howard W. Robertson

The Second of Seven
By: Jeremie Guy